POLICE ETHICS
Crisis in Law Enforcement

ABOUT THE AUTHOR

Dr. Tom Barker is the Dean of the College of Criminal Justice at Jacksonville State University in Jacksonville, Alabama. A former police officer and a certified police academy instructor, Dr. Barker has been conducting research on police corruption and police misconduct for over twenty years. He has written six books and over twenty articles on these topics. In addition, he has conducted numerous workshops and seminars for a variety of police agencies throughout the United States on ethical issues in law enforcement. Dr. Barker has served as an expert witness in both federal and state courts on police ethical behavior on numerous occasions.

Dr. Barker is a past president of the Academy of Criminal Justice Sciences (1987–1988) and the Southern Criminal Justice Association (1984–1985). He has received numerous awards including the Founders Award from both the Academy of Criminal Justice Sciences and the Southern Criminal Justice Association.

POLICE ETHICS

Crisis in Law Enforcement

By

TOM BARKER, PH.D.
Dean, College of Criminal Justice
Jacksonville State University
Jacksonville, Alabama

CHARLES C THOMAS • PUBLISHER
Springfield • Illinois • U.S.A.

Published and Distributed Throughout the World by
CHARLES C THOMAS • PUBLISHER
2600 South First Street
Springfield, Illinois 62794-9265

This book is protected by copyright. No part of
it may be reproduced in any manner without
written permission from the publisher.

© *1996 by* CHARLES C THOMAS • PUBLISHER
ISBN 0-398-06613-2 (cloth)
ISBN 0-398-06614-0 (paper)
Library of Congress Catalog Card Number: 96-3551

With THOMAS BOOKS *careful attention is given to all details of manufacturing
and design. It is the Publisher's desire to present books that are satisfactory as to their
physical qualities and artistic possibilities and appropriate for their particular use.*
THOMAS BOOKS *will be true to those laws of quality that assure a good name
and good will.*

Printed in the United States of America
SC-R-3

Library of Congress Cataloging-in-Publication Data

Barker, Tom.
    Police ethics : crisis in law enforcement / by Tom Barker.
      p.   cm.
    Includes bibliographical references and index.
    ISBN 0-398-06613-2 (cloth). — ISBN 0-398-06614-0 (paper)
    1. Police ethics—United States.   2. Law Enforcement—United
States.   I. Title.
HV7924.B37   1996
174'.93632—dc20   96-3551
                                                                           CIP

PREFACE

The objective of this book is to provide law enforcement officers and law enforcement supervisors with an understanding of ethical behavior as it relates to the police occupation. The author hopes that it will also serve as a training manual for new officers and as a refresher for experienced officers. If nothing else, the book should stimulate discussion of the ethical problems of the law enforcement community as we seek solutions for the current ethical crisis in law enforcement.

The book will examine four questions that are critical to the understanding of the ethical problems of the American law enforcement community. Those questions are: (1) Is law enforcement a profession? (2) Can law enforcement officers be professional? (3) What forms of behavior are the major law enforcement ethical violations? and (4) Can we control police ethical violations?

At times, the answer to these questions will be disturbing to some readers, particularly those who believe that rhetoric, denial, and blaming others are the solutions to the ethical crisis. Some will even deny that a crisis exists. However, the author believes one exists; many members of the public also believe a crisis exists and are expressing their displeasure in jury votes and calls for investigations. A substantial number of the professional law enforcement community believes there is an ethical crisis. The last group believes, as I do, that law enforcement is not going to become a profession just because we say it is. If American law enforcement is going to be recognized as a profession, we are going to have to ensure that the behavior of all law enforcement officers conforms to recognized ethical standards.

American law enforcement has standards of ethical behavior. We can use the *Law Enforcement Code of Ethics* as a model as we move to resolve the current crisis and seek to ensure that another one does not occur. The time for talk is over. Action, and action now, is needed.

CONTENTS

	Page
Preface	v
Chapter	
1. INTRODUCTION	3
2. LAW ENFORCEMENT CODE OF ETHICS—PARAGRAPH 1	9
3. LAW ENFORCEMENT CODE OF ETHICS—PARAGRAPH 2	15
4. LAW ENFORCEMENT CODE OF ETHICS—PARAGRAPH 3	19
5. LAW ENFORCEMENT CODE OF ETHICS—PARAGRAPH 4	23
6. WHAT FORMS OF BEHAVIOR ARE THE MAJOR LAW ENFORCEMENT ETHICAL VIOLATIONS?	25
7. CORRUPT PRACTICES	37
8. POLICE MISCONDUCT	43
9. CONTROL OF CORRUPTION AND MISCONDUCT	55
10. SUMMARY	77
Index	81

POLICE ETHICS
Crisis in Law Enforcement

Chapter 1

INTRODUCTION

The author believes that an understanding of the ethical problems of the American law enforcement community ultimately rests with the answer to four questions: Is law enforcement a profession? Can law enforcement officers be professional? What forms of behavior are the major law enforcement ethical violations? Can we control police ethical violations?

Is Law Enforcement a Profession?

If we are to accept the word of law enforcement spokespersons and read the "professional" law enforcement literature, the answer to this question would be an emphatic yes! The International Association of Chiefs Of Police (IACP), the professional voice of law enforcement, unequivocally states that law enforcement is a profession that:

- Is dedicated to the service of others.
- Requires personal commitment to service beyond the normal 8-hour day.
- Requires of its practitioners specialized knowledge and skills.
- Governs itself in relation to standards of admission, training and performance.
- Has mechanisms to ensure conformance and a disciplinary system to punish deviations.
- Forms associations to improve their collective ability to enhance service to others.
- Is guided by a code of ethics. (IACP, 1981)

I certainly agree with some of the IACP statements cited above, dedicated to the service of others, requires personal commitment beyond an 8-hour day, requires specialized skills and knowledge and forms associations. I could mount a strong argument against the statement that law enforcement "governs itself in relation to standards of admission, training and performance." The standards for admission range from "minimum" (I have always hated the use of this term in relation to police admission standards.) standards of 21, high school graduation or G.E.D., a driver's license, and no serious criminal record in some states to a baccalaureate degree at the federal level for special agent positions. The wide differences between training and performance standards among American law enforcement agencies are well known to all.

Does the law enforcement "profession" have "mechanisms to ensure conformance and a disciplinary system to punish deviations?" Some agencies do and some agencies don't. The mechanisms and systems work in some agencies and they don't in others. In my home state of Alabama, we have a system to certify law enforcement officers but no system to decertify. Therefore, we are in the embarrassing position of having several "certified" police officers in the penitentiary. One was on death row for some time, convicted of the murder of a fellow officer for her insurance. We certainly do not have a profession-wide system similar to the American Bar Association or the American Medical Association. The statement that the law enforcement "profession" "Is guided by a code of ethics" will be addressed later.

Whether or not one agrees that law enforcement is a profession, one has to agree that law enforcement as an occupation has come a long way since the establishment of the London Metropolitan Police in 1829. Furthermore, law enforcement in the United States has made tremendous strides since its transplant to New York City in 1884. The changes in law enforcement since I first "policed" in Birmingham, Alabama in the 1960s have been just a bit short of remarkable. But law enforcement will not be recognized as a profession just because we say it is.

Actually, the debate over whether or not law enforcement is a profession is best left to those who have the patience and time to argue theoretical and philosophical issues. I have neither. I thoroughly agree with Donald Witham, "reasonable and intelligent people could argue endlessly as to whether or not law enforcement meets all the characteristics of a profession (Witham, 1985:30). However, I also agree with Witham that as a practical matter no American occupational group has ever succeeded in having itself accepted as a profession without requiring the minimum educational standard of a baccalaureate degree (Witham, 1985:34).

I do not advocate that we give up on the law enforcement as a profession goal. It has been the goal of many police reformers and reform movements since the early 1900s, but "saying it is so ain't going to make it so." The goal may not have been realized, but there has been progress and it is still worth striving for. This leads us to the really important question—Can law enforcement officers be professional?

Can Law Enforcement Officers be Professional?

If we can all agree that the term professional is an adjective and refers to BEHAVIOR, the answer to this question is an emphatic and unequivocal—yes! That is, yes, if they know what they are doing, are proud of what they are doing, and if they prescribe to and follow a code of ethical behavior. At this time, we rely on the preservice and in-service training curriculums of the various law enforcement agencies at the local, state, and federal levels to ensure that law enforcement officers know what they are doing. To a degree, these same training centers or academies create a sense of pride in their trainees. This sense of pride is also dependent on the manner in which individual officers, groups of officers and the occupation, as a whole, prescribes to and follows a code of ethical behavior.

What is a code of ethical behavior? A *Code of Ethics,* according to *Webster's* is a code of behavior considered correct for a particular group, profession, or individual. A code of ethics is the rules and principles which govern the BEHAVIOR of that group, profession, or individual. The purpose of a code of ethics is to establish formal guidelines for ethical behavior and eliminate the ambiguity that surrounds individual considerations of what is right and wrong behavior (U.S. Department of Justice, 1978:16–22).

Does Law Enforcement need a Code of Ethics? Can a Code of Ethics promote ethical behavior? While some might jump to a quick answer to these questions and even argue that they are not worthy of debate, they need to be asked and examined. There is currently the public perception of an ethical crisis in American law enforcement. The existence of the Furman tapes in California is the latest indication of this crisis. Few in the law enforcement community would argue that Mark Fuhrman planted evidence at the Simpson crime scene; however, there appears to be ample evidence to believe that he lied on the stand concerning the use of the "N" word. We cannot blame the "Dream Team" in the "Circus in Los Angeles" for raising the specter of possible police misconduct, including the planting of evidence, as a defense in the O.J. Simpson trial. However, we may have to share the blame for the fact that so many people throughout the United States believed it. And, there is ample evidence to believe that the snap decision by the jury in that case was partly due to their belief that the issue of police misconduct raised a sufficient amount of reasonable doubt. Recent events throughout this country and not just in Los Angeles have cast serious doubts on the behavior of law enforcement officers.

There have been recent corruption scandals in New York City, New Orleans, Philadelphia, and Atlanta, to name a few. The Rodney King incident lead to the conviction of two police officers for civil rights violations. Two officers from Georgia have been tried for murder during this year. One was convicted and sentenced to two consecutive life terms plus five years. The furor surrounding the acquittal of the other Georgia officer forced the police chief to resign and the assistant chief and a major to be dismissed. Prosecutors in the latter case allege that potentially incriminating evidence was destroyed at the crime scene (*Law Enforcement News*, May 31, 1995:5). A Birmingham, Alabama former Police Officer of the Year was convicted of manslaughter for shooting a fleeing suspect in the back. He received a ten-year sentence. The Waco incident and Ruby Ridge fiasco have called into question the behavior of federal agencies and federal law enforcement officers. The Massachusetts Supreme Court recently cautioned judges regarding the possibility of police perjury and constitutional violations:

> Judges must zealously guard themselves against being used by police officers who lie and who violate constitutional rights in order to achieve what they improperly perceive as the greater end of convicting other wrong doers.
>
> (*Commonwealth v. Lewin*, 542 N.E. 2nd 275 Mass. 1989).

The litany of instances of unethical behavior by police officers could continue, including the instance where police officers stole money from the sale of Girl Scout cookies. However, there is little to be gained from this self flagellation. Suffice it to say that my twenty-five years of research into the topic of police deviance, has convinced me that it exists and is of sufficient quantity to be a real problem for law enforcement.

The debate over how representative the behaviors of the officers and departments cited above are of the 400,000+ law enforcement officers in this country could continue forever. It is simply a moot point. Debate over philosophical issues and pious and eloquent pronouncements and denials by members of the law enforcement community will not change the fact that sufficient evidence exists to more than suggest that unethical police behavior is a recurring and serious problem for law enforcement. The public and large numbers of hardworking, honest, and ethical police officers are ready for the law enforcement community to stop "talking the talk and start walking the walk."

We can stop blaming the media for creating the perception that police officers in some communities can not be trusted. We can stop blaming them for portraying only bad police behavior. That is what they do and they will continue to do it. We can stop blaming the politicians and the low pay and low status of the job. We, who are interested in ensuring ethical and lawful behavior for all police officers, should stop blaming everybody, including ourselves, and get about the business of promoting police ethical behavior.

The first step in the process of promoting police ethics is an examination of the current **Law Enforcement Code of Ethics.** Can it be used to rise above lofty ideal pronouncements more suited for saints and not us humans? Is it all talk and no substance? Does it have any practical value for street level police officers and hard pressed supervisors? Can it be used to promote and insure ethical police behavior? I will try to answer these questions.

THE LAW ENFORCEMENT CODE OF ETHICS

AS A LAW ENFORCEMENT OFFICER, MY FUNDAMENTAL DUTY IS TO SERVE THE COMMUNITY; TO SAFEGUARD LIVES AND PROPERTY; TO PROTECT THE INNOCENT AGAINST DECEPTION, THE WEAK AGAINST OPPRESSION OR INTIMIDATION, AND THE PEACEFUL AGAINST VIOLENCE OR DISORDER; AND TO RESPECT THE CONSTITUTIONAL RIGHTS OF ALL TO LIBERTY, EQUALITY AND JUSTICE.

I WILL KEEP MY PRIVATE LIFE UNSULLIED AS AN EXAMPLE TO ALL AND WILL BEHAVE IN A MANNER WHICH DOES NOT BRING DISCREDIT TO ME OR MY AGENCY. I WILL MAINTAIN COURAGEOUS CALM IN THE FACE OF DANGER, SCORN, OR RIDICULE; DEVELOP SELF RESTRAINT; AND BE CONSTANTLY MINDFUL OF THE WELFARE OF OTHERS. HONEST IN THOUGHT AND DEED IN BOTH MY PERSONAL AND OFFICIAL LIFE, I WILL BE EXEMPLARY IN OBEYING THE LAW AND THE REGULATIONS OF MY DEPARTMENT. WHATEVER I SEE OR HEAR OF A CONFIDENTIAL NATURE OR THAT IS CONFIDED TO ME IN MY OFFICIAL CAPACITY WILL BE KEPT EVER SECRET UNLESS REVELATION IS NECESSARY IN THE PERFORMANCE OF MY DUTY.

I WILL NEVER ACT OFFICIOUSLY OR PERMIT PERSONAL FEELINGS, PREJUDICES, POLITICAL BELIEFS, ASPIRATIONS, ANIMOSITIES OR FRIENDSHIPS TO INFLUENCE MY DECISIONS. WITH NO COMPROMISE FOR CRIME AND WITH RELENTLESS PROSECUTION OF CRIMINALS, I WILL ENFORCE THE LAW COURTEOUSLY AND APPROPRIATELY WITHOUT FEAR OR FAVOR, MALICE OR ILL WILL, NEVER EMPLOYING UNNECESSARY FORCE OR VIOLENCE AND NEVER ACCEPTING GRATUITIES.

I RECOGNIZE THE BADGE OF MY OFFICE AS A SYMBOL OF PUBLIC FAITH, AND I ACCEPT IT AS A PUBLIC TRUST TO BE HELD SO LONG AS I AM TRUE TO THE ETHICS OF POLICE SERVICE. I WILL NEVER ENGAGE IN ACTS OF BRIBERY NOR WILL I CONDONE SUCH ACTS BY OTHER POLICE OFFICERS. I WILL COOPERATE WITH ALL LEGALLY AUTHORIZED AGENCIES AND THEIR REPRESENTATIVES IN THE PURSUIT OF JUSTICE.

I KNOW THAT I ALONE AM RESPONSIBLE FOR MY OWN STANDARD OF PROFESSIONAL PERFORMANCE AND WILL TAKE EVERY OPPORTUNITY TO ENHANCE AND IMPROVE MY LEVEL OF KNOWLEDGE AND COMPETENCE.

I WILL CONSTANTLY STRIVE TO ACHIEVE THESE OBJECTIVES AND IDEALS, DEDICATING MYSELF BEFORE GOD TO MY CHOSEN PROFESSION...LAW ENFORCEMENT.

Chapter 2

LAW ENFORCEMENT CODE OF ETHICS— PARAGRAPH 1

AS A LAW ENFORCEMENT OFFICER, my fundamental duty is to serve mankind; to safeguard lives and property; to protect the innocent against deception, the weak against oppression or intimidation, and the peaceful against violation or disorder; and to respect the Constitutional rights of all men to liberty, equality and justice.

The **Law Enforcement Code of Ethics** begins with a series of ideal statements that may be hard for most mortals to live up to. They sound like something William Wallace, the Scottish hero of the movie **"Brave Heart,"** might have said. Should they be disregarded as guides for police ethical behavior? Do these ideal statements have any practical use for law enforcement? The answer to the first question is an emphatic no and the answer to the second question is an equally emphatic yes.

Before we begin our discussion, we should first define law enforcement officer, in order to identify those whom we believe are subject to the standards and rules of conduct contained in the **Code.** A law enforcement officer is any **public official,** who has the **extraordinary powers of arrest,** and he or his agency performs at least one of the three **direct police services** of patrol, traffic control, or criminal investigation (Barker, Hunter & Rush, 1994).

The term **public official** should not need any further definition. The **Code** applies only to public police officers who perform a service and not to private police who operate for the profit motive. The term **extraordinary powers of arrest** refers to those arrest powers granted by statute to public officials. We are referring to arrest powers that are above and beyond those possessed by all citizens in a democracy. Technically, all citizens in a democracy have citizen arrest powers. However, they are more limited and restricted than those granted to public officials who are paid to do full-time what is essentially every citizen's responsibility. We do not mean to imply that the arrest powers of law enforcement officers are not also limited and restricted, because they are. We will discuss these limitations and restrictions later.

The third element in our definition of law enforcement officer is that the agency or the officer performs one of the three **direct police services** of patrol, traffic control, and criminal investigation.

> **Patrol** is the organized surveillance of public places within a specified territory and response to reports of suspected criminal acts for the purpose of preventing crime, apprehending offenders, or maintaining public order. Officers on patrol also frequently respond to calls that are not crime-related.
>
> **Traffic Control** includes monitoring vehicular traffic and investigation of traffic accidents.
>
> **Criminal Investigation** is activity undertaken to identify alleged criminals, to gather evidence for criminal proceedings, or to recover stolen goods. (Ostrom, Parks, and Whitiker, 1978:24)

The definition does not imply that the agency or the officers must perform all three direct police services. Very few agencies above the local/municipal level would perform all three. However, they or their agency must perform one of the three. State Highway Patrol officers might only perform traffic control with a separate state agency responsible for criminal investigation, but they both would be law enforcement officers. The nonuniformed special agents for numerous criminal investigation agencies at all levels of government are all law enforcement officers. Some of the security officers for the Smithsonian Institution's Office of Protective Services perform patrol activities, often at fixed points in the museums. Others engage in only criminal investigation duties and still others perform traffic control duties. They are all by our definition law enforcement officers and subject to the **Code.** We must stop thinking of law enforcement officers as only uniformed police officers in local/municipal agencies.

Having defined those subject to the **Law Enforcement Code of Ethics,** we can now redirect our attention to the first paragraph. The three key concepts in this paragraph are **service, protect,** and **respect.** To serve and protect are familiar terms to the police. They are usually emblazoned on marked police vehicles. Countless number of police officers have sacrificed their lives in an effort to serve and protect the public.

As stated above, the law enforcement officer is first and foremost a public official. He or she works for some governmental entity whether at the local, county, state, or federal level. As a public official they have sworn an oath to serve and protect their cliental whether it be the visitors to the Smithsonian museums, the students on the campus of Jacksonville State University, the citizens of New York City, or the citizens of the United States as in the case of the Federal Bureau of Investigation.

Walker (1983) has stated that the three dominate features of policing can be traced back to our English heritage. They are:

1. **Limited authority**—The powers of the police are closely circumscribed by law.
2. **Local control**—The responsibility for providing police services rests primarily in local governments. While there are numerous variations within the United States regarding the organization of local, state, and federal law enforcement agencies, for the most part policing in the United States is highly decentralized and found in local agencies.
3. **Fragmented law enforcement**—The responsibility for providing police services, which is borne predominately by local agencies, is usually divided among several different agencies within an area. This often leads to problems with communication, cooperation and control among the agencies.

These features were incorporated into policing to protect citizens from the abuse of a strong state or federal government.

The law enforcement officer at any level of government is but one group of public officials that comprises our nation's formal means of social control—the Criminal Justice System. This system exists to accomplish four purposes: (1) control and prevent crime, (2) punish offenders, (3) treat and reform those amenable to such treatment, and (4) incapacitate those not amenable for treatment.

Law enforcement officers are in a sense the "gatekeepers" of this criminal justice system or process, if you will. Their outputs are the inputs to the other subsystems of the criminal justice system. They learn about crime from citizens, by discovery from officers in the field or through investigation and intelligence efforts. Once they verify that a crime has occurred, they must identify a suspect and, if possible, apprehend him or her for the criminal justice process to proceed (Barker, Hunter and Rush, 1994:22). However, if we examine the first paragraph of the **Code** we see that there is no specific mention of crime, crime prevention, making arrests, investigation, writing citations, running traffic or even the criminal justice system. That is because the police in a democracy while performing their crime-related duties have a higher calling or purpose.

The last sentence in the first paragraph of the **Code** "to respect the Constitutional rights of all men to liberty, equality and justice" is the essence of the law enforcement mission in a free society such as ours. The **National Advisory Commission on Criminal Justice Standards and Goals** in their report on the police stated, "If the overall purpose of the police service in America were narrowed to a single objective, that objective would be **to preserve the peace in a manner consistent with the freedoms secured by the Constitution**" (National Commission on Standards and Goals, 1973:13).

Law enforcement officers in a democratic society represent the most important protectors of individual and group liberties. They are vested with a significant amount of authority to restrict the free movement of persons and to lawfully subject citizens to embarrassment or indignity in the course of the investigation, search and/or arrest process (Barker and Carter, 1994). They have the right to use coercive force up to and including deadly force to effect these duties. Therefore, the misuse of their authority can and often does represent the greatest threat to the individual and group liberties they are to protect.

The police in a free society, such as ours, have a hard task to perform. They must perform their duties and exercise their authority within the constraints of the law. No action that they take is not subject to review for its own legality. The familiar names of **Mapp, Miranda, Escobedo, Schmerber** represent Supreme Court decisions which restricted police actions in dealing with citizens. Although recent Supreme Court decisions, such as **Terry v. Ohio, U.S. v. Leon, Chimel v. California, Hester v. U.S.,** to name a few, may have relaxed some restrictions on law enforcement behavior; they were also decided on Constitutional and not crime control issues.

The fear of governmental abuse and zealous protection of civil liberties and individual rights embodied in our Constitution and the Bill of Rights will always interfere with the crime control efforts of law enforcement agencies. However, that is the way our forefathers and countless generations of Americans wanted it. We are willing to tolerate greater amounts of crime and criminality to protect our individual freedoms. We, as a free society, will not tolerate a law enforcement agency staffed by **Dirty Harrys,** who use illegal and unethical means to accomplish what they perceive as legitimate ends. We will always closely examine the means to which the ends of law enforcement were accomplished. Furthermore, we will always depend on law enforcement officers who prescribe to the **Law Enforcement Code of Ethics** to "respect the Constitutional rights of all men to liberty, equality and justice."

Chapter 3

LAW ENFORCEMENT CODE OF ETHICS— PARAGRAPH 2

I WILL keep my private life unsullied as an example to all; maintain courageous calm in the face of danger, scorn or ridicule; develop self restraint; and be constantly mindful of the welfare of others. Honest in thought and deed in both my personal and official life, I will be exemplary in obeying the laws of the land and the regulations of my department. Whatever I see or hear of a confidential nature or that is confided to me in my official capacity will be kept ever secret unless revelation is necessary in the performance of my duty.

In this paragraph there are two references to an officer's private life; I will keep my private life unsullied as an example to all, honest in thought and deed in both my personal and official life. Should an officer's private life be subject to review and scrutiny? Before we answer that question, we should consider that a law enforcement officer or cop, if you will, is an example of what is known as a master status.

A status is the social position we occupy in a group. And, we all occupy several social positions in various groups. For example, I occupy the social positions of College Dean, professor, police academy instructor, expert witness, husband, father, etc. A master status is one that cuts across all the statuses that you may hold and comes to be the one that you are known by and, often, the standard that identifies your expected behavior. As you can imagine, the master status that most often is used to describe me is College Dean. A master status often literally takes over and controls one's identity. It conjures up a mental image for most people and its "wearer" is always judged in relation to it.

Some master statuses once held are held for life. The bearer only becomes an "ex", e.g., ex-marine, ex-cop, ex-con, ex-pro in sports, ex-prizefighter, etc. Consider how many times Lee Harvey Oswald and Charles Whitman, the mass murderer in the bell tower at the University of Texas at Austin, were referred to, and are still being referred to as ex-Marines. Yet, neither of these two assassins spent more than a short tour in the Marine Corps. Tony Danza, the actor, is still being referred to as an ex-prizefighter, although he had a modest 13-3 record many years ago. If a person goes to the penitentiary, no matter how long they live, they will be known and referred to as ex-con. The same applies to cops. After you are no longer a cop, you will simply become an ex-cop for life.

Given that your cop master status defines your identity and is used as the standard to judge the appropriateness or inappropriateness of your behavior, we should return to our question concerning a law enforcement officer's personal life. Should it be subject to review and scrutiny? Actually, the answer to that question is really academic. Whether or not it should or should not be, it is subject to review and scrutiny by the public because law enforcement is a master status. Therefore, the law enforcement officer should (I will not go as far to say "will") strive to keep his or her private life unsullied as an example to all. The officer who is known to drink excessively, gamble, or not pay his debts will be judged more harshly by those who know him or her. If he or she is known to be a liar, his or her court testimony will be held in question. If the officer is known to be abusive to family members, those who know him or her will always wonder how they can impartially handle domestic disturbances on the job. The officer who drinks and drives will be viewed as a hypocrite by those who know that he or she arrests nonpolice for the same offense. It just cannot be avoided; once the officer pins on the badge and takes the oath, his or her private life comes under the microscope.

The law enforcement officer should be honest in thought. However, we must recognize that even former president (How about that for a master status?) Jimmy Carter admitted to having "lust in his heart." Keeping our thoughts honest at all times may be impossible to accomplish. However, we should not budge an inch from demanding that all law enforcement officers are honest in deed both in their personal and official life. Integrity is just too important to being a professional law enforcement officer that it cannot be compromised in either the officer's personal or official life.

Maintaining calm in the face of danger, scorn, or ridicule, and developing self-restraint are noble principles to ascribe to. The overwhelming majority of law enforcement officers in this country adhere to these principles. One only has to compare the police handling of "anti-everything" disturbances from abortion to gay rights demonstrations and protests in recent years to what was common during the "police riots" of the sixties. Although there have been some bad examples of dealing with demonstrations and protests in recent years, the law enforcement community as a whole is doing a much better job than in previous years.

Obviously, we would expect that law enforcement officers would obey the laws of the land and the regulations of his or her department. We would also expect that confidential information that comes to the officer by way of his or her official position would be kept secret. Friends, acquaintances, and even relatives sometimes ask law enforcement officers for information on cases or people who have been arrested. The majority of the time the officer being questioned will know nothing about the case or the person. Citizens do not seem to understand that they may have more information from media sources than the officer has. However, on occasion the officer is privy to the requested information. It should be kept confidential. Most people understand that those who tell secrets cannot be trusted to keep secrets. The officer who gossips or reveals confidential information will soon acquire the reputation of being untrustworthy.

Chapter 4

LAW ENFORCEMENT CODE OF ETHICS— PARAGRAPH 3

I WILL never act officiously or permit personal feelings, prejudices, animosities or friendships to influence my decisions. With no compromise for crime and with relentless prosecution of criminals, I will enforce the law courteously and appropriately without fear or favor, malice or ill will, never employing unnecessary force or violence and never accepting gratuities.

The first sentence of this paragraph makes clear that law enforcement officers who prescribe to the **Code** should always remember they are not the law. They are only paid full time to enforce the law. Their duties should never become personal. The "avenging angel syndrome," where officers exact their sense of street justice on individuals and groups they personally dislike, is to be avoided at all costs. We expect law enforcement officers to be even-handed in the execution of their duties. However, all law enforcement officers are human beings and because of that, they will have personal feelings. They will have buttons that if pushed will make them mad. It is often said that most people go to jail or get citations for "contempt of cop"—COC. Not showing the proper respect or challenging the officer's authority will get you in jail or a ticket quick according to this concept. The professional law enforcement officer will rise above the need to ensure respect through his or her arrest powers. His or her discretionary powers should not be exercised for personal reasons no matter how strong.

The law enforcement officer can, and does, exercise a tremendous amount of discretion and, particularly for nonserious misdemeanors or traffic citations, there is no need to put everyone in jail who violates the law or give a ticket to everyone who commits a traffic infraction. There are numerous situations where warnings, counseling, or a word of advice are a better choice of action than arrest or citation. Chiefs and sheriffs are continually reminding me that police academies do a good job of telling "rookies" when to make an arrest. However, the academies fail at telling police officers when *not* to make an arrest.

The rigid personality who feels that he or she must enforce all criminal and traffic violations will never become a true professional law enforcement officer. Those officers who proudly announce that they would give their own wife or mother a ticket if they saw them break a traffic law are either liars or fools, maybe both. They are also not the officers we want answering domestic disturbance calls or handling protests or, for that matter, any police action that requires tact and judgement. In this country selective enforcement of traffic laws is the norm. Selective enforcement is the only practical approach to traffic enforcement. Full enforcement of the law, particularly traffic laws, is neither logical, practical, and not really wanted by the citizens. The officer must adhere to the principle of reasonableness in making his or her decisions. They must consider the total situation and what is the end they want to attain with their action. I remember years ago, working a major college football game, when my young partner asked if we were going to arrest all the drunks. I told him that I didn't know where we would put them all. The city jail would not hold them. I also told him I thought the city would have to call in the National Guard to handle the ensuing riot. We did make some arrests that day, but we certainly did not arrest all the drunks in the football stadium. I could recite other instances where I or the officers I worked with did not arrest or ticket someone who broke the law or a traffic regulation, but that is not necessary. Every working law enforcement officer can recite numerous instances from his or her own experiences.

We will discuss the issue of unnecessary use of force fully later. However, we should all recognize at this time that the unnecessary use of force by police officers is certainly not consistent with our definition of a professional law enforcement officer.

The **Code** is very explicit on the acceptance of gratuities. It says that law enforcement officers will never accept gratuities. It does not say those over a certain monetary amount. It does not indicate if there is a difference between systematic and incidental gratuities. The **Code** does not mention the intent of the giver or the effect on the officer's behavior. There is no mention of the acceptance of gratuities as a possible "grey area" of corruption. These questions will all be addressed more fully later. Two issues that I will raise at this time are the effect of police acceptance of gratuities, no matter how small, on those who observe officers in uniform receiving free cups of coffee or discount meals and how those who give these favors to the police may view it.

Those having to pay for their coffee and full price for their meals may not hold a very high opinion of their public servants receiving free coffee and discounted meals. They probably will not be sympathetic to police demands for pay raises and increased benefits. I have often heard the following comment from citizens and even council members who were in the position of voting on police pay raises: "Why should we give the police more money, they get everything they want free or discounted now?" It is hard to argue against this statement in an area where it is well known that the giving and accepting of small and large gratuities by law enforcement officers is common practice. Some are even more animate in their description of their public servants when they refer to them as "free loading sons of a bitch."

Now to the issue of the perception of those who give these favors to the police. When discussing this issue in the Police Academy, I always relate the following personal experience. While I was working undercover, I stopped in a well-known fast food restaurant; the identity will remain anonymous, but I guarantee you there is one in every city I have been in and they are well known for giving police free or discounted meals and drinks. It was closing time when I ordered my Coke® and cheeseburger. While waiting at the counter for my order, I observed the following. There was a tray of unsold and unwrapped hamburgers and cheeseburgers laying on the table in the back. One of the young high school-aged workers picked up the tray and emptied it in the garbage. The manager, on seeing her do this, screamed, "Don't throw them away; we always give them to the precinct." At this point, the manager and the young worker picked the hamburgers and cheeseburgers out of the garbage and wrapped them and put them in a large carry-out sack. A few seconds later, a smiling uniformed officer came in and was given the sack. The manager smiled and told him, "Tell the guys to enjoy." I followed the police car to the precinct and was able to tell the hungry officers what had happened before they ate the filthy meal. It then took me about fifteen minutes to talk them out of going back there and putting the manager in jail. I told them that the publicity would make them look bad and probably give other restaurant owners some bad ideas. The last comment convinced them to cease and desist. However, I can only imagine what may have happened to the manager and the restaurant later.

Chapter 5

LAW ENFORCEMENT CODE OF ETHICS— PARAGRAPH 4

I RECOGNIZE the badge of my office as a symbol of public faith, and I accept it as a public trust to be held so long as I am true to the ethics of police service. I will never engage in acts of bribery nor will I condone such acts by other police officers. I will cooperate with all legally authorized agencies and their representatives in the pursuit of justice.

While it may be true that all social relationships are based on trust, there is a special trust embodied in the law enforcement badge. We, in our interactions with others, trust them to behave in appropriate and accepted fashion. Society is based on this principle. We "trust" others to be honest, truthful, and respectful of our feelings in their dealings with us. We "trust" that others will treat us as persons and not objects. We "trust" that parents will take care of their children. We "trust" that people will pay their debts.

In some people we place more "trust" than others. We "trust" that our husbands and wives will not violate their marriage vows. We "trust" that our children will obey our wishes. We "trust" our friends and relatives. We all know people who claim not to "trust" anyone and we in turn do not "trust" them. I put trust in quotes because we all know that not all persons act in appropriate and acceptable ways. That is why societies have forms of deviant (or norm violating) behavior all the way from inappropriate social behavior (picking one's nose at the table, not observing standards of personal hygiene, overuse of certain words of profanity, talking in church, etc.) to crime. Societies have formal and informal means of social control to control and discipline those who do not act appropriately. We rely on social groups to enforce the informal means of social control. The criminal justice system exists to control and punish those who violate those behaviors considered serious enough to be enacted into law.

The law enforcement officer, as the most visible representative of the formal social control system and our representative of the democracy we live in, is given a special trust. He or she, after taking their oath of office, is given the badge as a symbol of that trust. Because of the authority we give them, we expect that they will always engage in lawful and ethical behavior. We also expect them to not condone unlawful and unethical behavior by other law enforcement officers. This special relationship we have with our law enforcement officers is what makes their unethical behavior so serious and disturbing. The professional law enforcement officer who adheres to the **Law Enforcement Code of Ethics** recognizes and understands this special relationship.

> I **KNOW** that I alone am responsible for my own standard of professional performance and will take every opportunity to enhance and improve my level of knowledge and competence.

This paragraph reinforces the principle that professional performance and adherence to the **Code** is a personal commitment. The devil or the peer group (other law enforcement officers) cannot be blamed for violations of the **Code.** The law enforcement officer will have to accept personal responsibility for his or her unethical behavior. He or she will have to accept personal responsibility for condoning the unethical behavior of others that they are aware of.

This paragraph also makes clear that professional development in the field of law enforcement is also a personal commitment. The professional law enforcement officer will take advantage of every opportunity to enhance his or her knowledge and competence in the field of law enforcement. The department also shares in this responsibility. They have the duty to provide a continuous process of training throughout the officer's career.

> I **WILL** constantly strive to achieve these objectives and ideals, dedicating myself before GOD to my chosen profession . . . LAW ENFORCEMENT.

Chapter 6

WHAT FORMS OF BEHAVIOR ARE THE MAJOR LAW ENFORCEMENT ETHICAL VIOLATIONS?

The major violations of the **Law Enforcement Code of Ethics** are police corruption and other forms of police misconduct. *Police corruption* is defined as the misuse of the officer's official position for actual or expected reward or gain (Barker and Roebuck, 1973). According to this definition the officer must **misuse** (do something that he or she should not do, or fail to do something he or she should do) his or her official position. Corrupt acts can occur off duty if that act is somehow related to the officer's employment as a sworn police officer. For example, the officer could learn of confidential information related to an individual and convey this information to that individual or another while off duty. The officer could also, during his or her normal patrol duties, "case" businesses for possible robberies or burglaries. In a less serious vein, the officer could solicit a "police discount" while off duty.

Whatever the officer receives through the misuse of his or her authority must be of some **material reward** or **gain.** Material reward or gain must be some tangible object, either cash, services, or goods that have cash value. This requirement will allow us to draw an important distinction between corruption and misconduct. In addition, police corruption will violate a law, ethical standard, or a work rule and regulation. As we shall see, most acts of corruption will violate all three.

In the past, this definition has been accused of being too legalistic, because it requires a concrete actual or expected material reward or gain. Others would add in vague terms such as social or political gain, enhanced status, prestige, and some even prejudice and favoritism. Others would only confine police corruption to bribery or money corruption. Obviously, all acts of bribery will be corrupt, but not all corruption is bribery. Most will involve money, but some will not. As we shall see, not all corruption involves money corruption. Some have overgeneralized the concept to include police brutality and discrimination. This overgeneralization only confuses the area.

My prior background as a police officer actually influenced the decision to confine the definition of police corruption to those acts where there was a material reward or gain. In all criminal cases, that I am aware of, one must present evidence, either concrete or circumstantial, to prove the case. Furthermore, there must be some act that accompanies the intent. Intent by itself is not sufficient. The presence of a material reward or gain represents the concrete evidence of a corrupt act. The showing that the officer misused his official position in either not doing something he or she was required to do, or doing something that they were not supposed to do, in exchange for that material reward or gain, in my opinion, completes the definition. I never could, and still cannot, determine how one could satisfactorily demonstrate that the officer received social or political gain, enhanced status, or prestige. Loose or vague definitions are not very useful for those who are trying to make practical decisions to determine if theirs or others' behaviors are corrupt. I can just imagine an internal affairs officer going to the chief and accusing an officer of a corrupt act that enhanced that officer's status or prestige.

There are at least eight patterns or types of police behavior that can be classified as corruption.

Patterns of Police Corruption

Corruption of Authority

Corruption of Authority involves the officer receiving free meals, liquor, services (e.g., free wrecker/towing services, free legal advice, etc.), free admission to entertainment, or rewards. As you can see, I purposely omitted free coffee from the definition. It is not because I do not think that free coffee should be included. I do. I left it out because, through the years, I have spent countless number of hours arguing with individual and groups of officers on this issue. There seems to be the idea among many law enforcement officers that there is some kind of "divine right" to free coffee for cops. Even though I have tried to point out that the **Code** says "never accepting gratuities" and many of the officers' own departments had rules and regulations forbidding the acceptance of any gratuities, there were still arguments. The answer to this has always been, "but they did not mean 'free coffee.'" Remember what I said about not having the time or the patience to argue theoretical and philosophical issues. I feel the same way about arguing with people who are convinced of their position and will not be swayed by facts or reason. For that reason, I have come to the conclusion to omit free coffee from the definition, with the statement that if that was all we had to worry about, then law enforcement was in good ethical shape. I have told these officers to drink all the free coffee they want if they think it is not included in the **Code**'s definition of gratuities or, maybe, their own department's definition of gratuities. I have also pointed out that if the department had a rule forbidding free coffee and the officer accepted the same, they, meaning the department, always had a way to discipline them, including firing them for breaking a rule or regulation. The excuse that everybody does it may not work at a departmental or civil service hearing. Nevertheless, I will never budge on free or discounted meals or any other supposed "fringe benefits" of the job being included in the pattern—Corruption of Authority.

As you can readily see, all the behaviors included in the definition outlined above involve "respectable citizens" who may be "freely" giving "gifts" to their police officers. Some may not expect anything in return. Or maybe we should say that they did not expect anything in return when the gift was offered. At the time the gratuity is offered and accepted, neither party may expect the officer to misuse his or her position. However, at a later date such "respectable citizen" or one of their employees, relatives, or friends may get a ticket, be arrested for a "nonserious" misdemeanor, need help with a licensing agency, or they may want the officer to look-up somebody for a possible record check. Who are they going to call for help? In all probability, they are going to call the officers who have accepted their gratuities.

The officer/s are now in a difficult situation. They can wax indignant on not compromising their official position, say there is nothing they can do (which is probably true), promise to try to help in order to "cool" them out, or they may actually find a way to help their benefactor, even if it means compromising their position or that of another officer. In any event, acceptance of the gratuity, no matter how small, has the potential of compromising the officer's authority and affecting his or her ability to discharge their duties equitably. Furthermore, Article 9 of the **Canons of Police Ethics** specifically addresses these behaviors.

Article 9. Gifts and Favors. The law enforcement officer, representing government bears the heavy responsibility of maintaining, in his own conduct, the honor and integrity of all government institutions. He shall, therefore, guard against placing himself in a position which any person can expect special consideration or in which the public can reasonably assume that special consideration is being given. *Thus, he should be firm in refusing gifts, favors, or gratuities, large or small, which can, in the public mind, be interpreted as capable of influencing his judgement in the discharge of his duties.* (IACP, 1981. Italics added)

As you can see, the article cited above goes much farther than the **Code.** All doubt is removed and there is a clear expectation that the officer will not accept gifts, favors, or gratuities, large or small. It also points out that behavior that creates the impression that the officer has been compromised should be avoided. As we learned early in life from our parents, avoid evil and the appearance of evil.

In 1983, the State of Alabama's Ethics Commission issued an advisory opinion on free meals. Part of that opinion follows:

> Any law enforcement agent or officer coming under the Ethics law who accepts a free meal or cut-rate meal with the understanding that he will devote more of his time to insuring protection for the restaurant or eating establishment to a greater degree than another restaurant which does not offer free or cut-rate meals violates Section 36-25-6 of the Alabama Ethics law . . .

At the time this advisory opinion was rendered, the argument was raised among some law enforcement groups that free meals or cut-rate meals were only unethical if there was an understanding that the officer would devote more time to protecting these eating establishments over those who do not. Therefore, no understanding or intention on the part of the officers to do this, then no ethical violation. Two years ago an incident happened in Alabama which proved explicitly what I had been maintaining was always implied in such arrangements.

An irate citizen complained to the city council of one of the municipalities about city police officers receiving free and discounted meals from one of the fast food chains. Her complaint named a particular restaurant and its location. The complaint received wide media coverage. A police captain, identified by name in the newspaper, was quoted as saying, "you could not buy a police officer from his department with a free hamburger." According to the newspaper, he went on to say that the woman who complained was a troublemaker and there was nothing wrong with police officers receiving free or discounted meals.

This last comment caused me to write one of the two letters to the editor I have ever written. In my letter, which was published, I stated that there was something wrong with police officers accepting free or discounted meals. I pointed out that the **Law Enforcement Code of Ethics,** as well as the captain's own department, prohibited such behavior. I raised other ethical issues in my letter also and suggested that if law enforcement officers could not live by the **Code,** then it should be changed. I pointed out that his department had a rule against accepting *any* gratuities. I thought that should be changed also if he and his department thought there was nothing wrong with accepting free or discounted meals. I also stated that there were numerous professional police officers who did not agree with this captain. The matter was closed, I thought.

Several weeks after my letter was printed, this very fast food restaurant and a number of customers were robbed by a group of "gang bangers" from a nearby metropolitan area. An unnamed police captain was quoted in the media as saying, "If they hadn't stopped the free meals, there would probably have been a cop in there when it happened." In my opinion, that statement is pure and simple extortion. No free meals, no protection.

Other officers in other cities have also sanctioned businesses and others who have refused to give the "perks" of the job. They have excluded businesses from routine security checks, customers have been harassed, citations have been issued for obscure and seldom enforced violations, and private and business property has even been sabotaged.

The Alabama Ethics Commission in the same advisory opinion cited above made another statement that I wholeheartedly agree with:

> . . . . The Commission would find no unethical implications if **all** public employees were given discounts on meals in order to increase business by establishments, but to single out only those individuals who happen to carry a badge is difficult to understand even when done under the guise of tradition. (Alabama Ethics Commission, July 6, 1983)

It is difficult to understand why only law enforcement officers are selected for these "perks," and even harder to justify no matter what rationalization is offered. I learned in graduate school that man is not a rational animal. He is a rationalizing animal. Whenever he does something that he believes is wrong, he will find a rationalization or excuse for that behavior. Every police officer who has been on the street for over a year knows this; think of the rationalizations or excuses that have come from those you have arrested. The most frequent one, I suspect, is "I was drunk." Even child molesters will tell how the young girl enticed them. Some murderers will explain that the victim asked for it or had it coming.

Some police officers come up with simple rationalizations for the violations of the **Code** that occur under **Corruption of Authority** and the other patterns of corruption and misconduct. Examples of these rationalizations or excuses are: police work is a low paying job; they are just fringe benefits, "perks" of the job; these people like the police; everybody does it; if you don't do it, nobody will trust you; etc. These statements should be recognized for what they are, rationalizations and excuses for behavior that the officer knows is wrong. If a police officer has to ask himself or herself if the behavior is wrong, then you can bet it is.

Some still debate that the behaviors described above are not corrupt acts and they do not adversely affect the actions of police officers (Kania, 1988). In fact, they use rationalizations cited above as the justification for their argument.

> Like most police officers who have completed a modern, progressive police academy program I knew the conventional ethical standard obliged me to forgo taking any gratuities. When I arrived on the street, paired with a veteran officer, I was quickly shown that the **supposed** unethical behavior was the social norm for the police and the merchants alike (Kania, 1988 Italics added).

Kania even goes on to suggest that police officers should be encouraged to accept gifts from members of the community in order to build a closer working relationship between the police and their communities (Kania, 1988:39). I would argue that using the rationalization that it is the "social norm for the police and the merchants" (everybody does it) does not obviate the fact that accepting gratuities is prohibited by the **Code.** The "conventional ethical standard" that he learned in the police academy did not become "supposed unethical behavior" when he got to the street just because everybody, the police and the merchants, was doing it.

Kickbacks

Although some may dispute that the behaviors described in **"Corruption of Authority"** are corrupt acts, I would expect few to argue that the behaviors to be described in **kickbacks** are not examples of police corruption. They will all involve the misuse of the officer's official position for a material reward or gain. **Kickbacks** are money, goods, and services accepted from such "legitimate" businesses and individuals as towing companies, ambulances, garages, lawyers, doctors, undertakers, taxicabs, service stations, moving companies, etc.

All the businesses or individuals cited above have something to gain from a good working relationship with their local police. Many of the business people listed above freely distribute their cards to police officers and indicate their willingness to "take care of the officer" if they receive referrals from the officer. The "ambulance chasing" lawyer may pay a police officer for all referrals. Police officers, especially those who investigate traffic accidents, are in a good position to suggest an attorney for a possible liability suit. Towing companies and automobile repair and body shops are highly competitive businesses that can benefit from a good working relationship with one or more police officers. In fact, most police agencies have established a rotating list of wrecker services to avoid the possibility of corrupt arrangements.

Some police assignments have more potential for **kickbacks** than others. For example, accident investigation, especially those units that investigate serious injuries and fatalities which almost always result in civil litigation (lawyer-police conspiracy), complaint desk assignments (lawyers, bondsman-police conspiracy), bonds details (bondsman-police conspiracy).

Opportunistic Thefts

The behavior patterns to be discussed are unique because they do not involve corruptors. **Opportunistic thefts** occur when police officers steal money or other valuables from those they arrest or from crime victims. Also included in this pattern of corruption are thefts from crime scenes and unprotected property. The "rolled" arrestee, traffic accident victims, and unconscious or dead citizens are unaware of the corrupt act.

Officers who engage in these behaviors do not, in all likelihood, begin their shifts with the intention of stealing something; however, the opportunity presents itself under a low-risk situation and a theft occurs. I heard years ago that a good explanation of criminality is "The opportunity and the inclination come together under a low-risk situation." The officers committing these thefts already have the inclination; all they need is the opportunity and what they perceive to be a low-risk situation.

Perhaps an officer is called to or discovers a business that has been burglarized and decides to take some of the merchandise or money left behind by the first thief. On occasion, police officers have taken money or valuables from unconscious or dead crime victims, particularly those who were involved in illegal activities, e.g., a drug dealer shot while involved in a drug transaction. Police officers making routine business checks may find a door unlocked or some other unsecured property and decide to take something. These behaviors are obviously corrupt and examples of criminal activities by police officers. By definition they are a violation of the **Code.** Unfortunately, they occur in some police departments.

Sometimes individuals who have a propensity for these acts are also well known. I was teaching a class on police ethics some years ago when an officer in the class made the comment, "We have an officer in our department whom you would not want investigating a traffic accident that you or a member of your family was involved in." Several other members of the class joined in and one even mentioned the officer by name. When I asked why they did not do something about him, they all replied, "Damn, Doc, you know why we don't." I sure did. They felt some strange sense of loyalty to this officer because he was a cop. They also did not want to be known as snitches. I told them that there were no "honest cops" watching "dishonest cops" commit crimes. I also told them that I believed that law enforcement would never be a profession as long as "some cops had their hands in other people's pockets and other cops knew about it and did nothing." I will return to this more fully later.

Shakedowns

Shakedowns involve police officers extorting money or other valuables from criminals, usually caught in the act, or traffic offenders. These forms of behavior often arise opportunistically, i.e., the officer inadvertently witnesses or gains knowledge of a criminal violation and violator and accepts a bribe for not making an arrest. Shakedowns are usually engaged in with little fear of being caught because the victims are unlikely to complain since he or she is engaged in some illegal activity.

Officers will take bribes from transporters of contraband such as gambling paraphernalia or pornography, bootleg liquor or cigarettes, or traffic violators. We have all read accounts of police officers taking money or dope from drug dealers caught in the act of transporting or dealing dope. The New York City Police Department's "Buddy Boys" is a good example of this pattern of corruption (McAlary, 1987). The modern-day police officer in a large urban city may sooner or later be presented with a situation where he or she is exposed to temptations unheard of in the past. This has to be realized and discussed. All law enforcement officers must face the issue. We do not want them to face the temptation of huge sums of money without having some idea of what they might do or should do. Fortunately, most will make the right and the ethical decision; however, some will yield to the temptation and a small number are waiting for the opportunity to arise. This latter group will seek out opportunities to shake down criminals and traffic violators.

In the area of traffic violators, virtually all uniformed police officers have numerous opportunities to shakedown those they stop for traffic offenses. The serious consequences associated with DUI arrests and convictions have introduced a new potential for corrupt activities.

COSTS OF A DUI SHAKEDOWN
INTOXICATED DRIVER PAYS OFFICER $50.00 TO FORGET VIOLATION

COST TO CITY	LOSS OF FINE, LOSS OF CREDIBILITY IN TRAFFIC ENFORCEMENT, DAMAGE TO CITY'S REPUTATION.
COST TO DRIVER	AMOUNT OF FUTURE SHAKEDOWNS, INCREASED LIKELIHOOD THAT HE WILL BE STOPPED IN FUTURE, POSSIBILITY OF BEING PROSECUTED, INCREASED RISK OF DEATH AND INJURY
COSTS TO OTHER DRIVERS	INCREASED RISK OF DEATH OR INJURY FROM RELEASED OFFENDER, INCREASED LIKELIHOOD THEY WILL BE STOPPED IN HOPES THEY CAN BE SHAKEN DOWN FOR A BRIBE.
COSTS TO THE PUBLIC	INCREASED RISKS OF DEATH AND INJURY, INCREASED INSURANCE RATES, JUSTICE ONLY FOR THOSE WHO CAN PAY
COSTS TO POLICE AGENCY	DAMAGE TO REPUTATION, LOSS OF CONFIDENCE IN AGENCY, LOSS OF INDIVIDUAL OFFICER'S CREDIBILITY

Protection of Illegal Activities

If I asked each of you reading this manuscript to give an example of police corruption, most of you would have given an example from this pattern of behavior. **Protection of Illegal Activities** refers to those forms of behavior where law enforcement officers receive protection money or other valuables from vice operators or legitimate companies who operate illegally. So-called victimless crimes, including vice operations related to gambling, illegal drug sales, prostitution, liquor violations, pornography rings, and after hours clubs, can increase their profits and decrease their risks through a good working relationship with the police. Unfortunately, there has been a long history of collusion between police and vice operators in many American cities.

Protection money or goods can also come from legitimate companies that operate illegally. Law enforcement officers have control over numerous businesses that are restricted by license and the law. For example, taxicabs, restaurants, trucking firms, bars, liquor stores, pharmacies, pawnshops, and gun dealers are all regulated by the law. These companies or businesses, some more than others, have paid tribute to the police to operate outside the range of their licenses or other restrictions: for example, a bar that stays open after hours or serves liquor or food for which they do not have a license or a taxicab that operates outside prescribed routes or picks up or discharges fares at unauthorized sites.

There has also been a long tradition in some urban cities of construction companies paying police officers to overlook violations of city regulations, e.g., trucks blocking traffic, violating pollution guidelines, and blocking sidewalks.

The increased specialization brought about by attempts to professionalize police departments has created a situation where it is not necessary to pay off members of an entire police organization to insure protection. Only the detail that handles the relevant activity—cab detail, safe burglary, drug unit, vice detail, etc.—must be paid off.

Fixes

There are two behavior patterns included within the **fix:** the quashing of misdemeanor or felony prosecutions and the disposal of traffic tickets. This form of bribery involves the officer taking something of value to "fix" a case or a traffic ticket. Obviously, it would be easier for the uniformed officer to fix misdemeanor cases or tickets than to fix a felony prosecution. He or she would have more control over misdemeanor cases or tickets. In a felony prosecution, the matter would be handled by a detective or someone from the prosecutor's office. The detective/s would be in a better position for a felony fix. Obviously, prior to or at the preliminary hearing is the optimum period to fix a criminal case; should the case proceed to the grand jury or trial court stage, it becomes more difficult and more expensive to fix a case.

When the "fix is in," the investigating officer agrees to "sell the case," that is withdraw prosecution. He or she either fails to request prosecution, tampers with the existing evidence, or gives perjured testimony. He or she can also say that they failed to do something they were required to do, such as giving the **Miranda Warning** or securing a search warrant.

It is becoming extremely difficult to fix traffic tickets as more and more states move to serially numbered uniform traffic citations. There has to be some explanation given for a missing or rescinded ticket. Nevertheless, this has not stopped ticket fixing by some officers.

Direct Criminal Activities

All forms of police corruption past **Corruption of Authority** are serious ethical violations and crimes; however, this pattern of behavior is particularly grave. Police officers actively engage in such crimes as robbery, burglary, and the sale and trafficking in narcotics in this pattern. These officers are crooks in uniform. When I first began conducting research on police corruption, I would never have believed that law enforcement officers would become involved in drug-related corruption to the extent that some have today.

A recent federal indictment named a Washington, D.C. police officer as a leading "supplier, owner and leader" of a heroin distribution operation in Philadelphia (*Law Enforcement News*, September 15, 1991, p. 5). Unfortunately, the huge profits available in drug trafficking has lead to a large number of corrupt activities on the part of law enforcement officers at all levels of government.

However, some police officers engage in direct criminal activities unrelated to drugs. In 1990, a Belle Glade, Florida police officer was arrested and charged with burglarizing a Catholic church (*Law Enforcement News*, October 15, 1990, p. 2). At the time of his arrest he had burglar's tools and $3,000 allegedly stolen from the church. How low can you go? A former partner of mine used to say, "There is no need to check churches. God will take care of those low enough to break into a church." Unfortunately, in my seventeen years of teaching in the police academy, I have had "rookies" in my classes who were later convicted of crimes ranging from murder to robbery. I will quickly add that I also have had "rookies" in those same classes who have and are still leading ethical and honest careers as professional law enforcement officers. Sadly to say, there were officers in those classes who gave their lives in service to their communities. The "damn" crooks who sat in those classes with them dishonored them and the entire law enforcement occupation.

Internal Payoffs

This is also a unique form of police corruption because the corruptors and corruptees are law enforcement officers. Police officers "sell" work assignments, off-days, holidays, evidence, and promotions to each other. An officer would approach his or her supervisor and request a change in work assignment and suggest a money figure, or the supervisor might tell the officer how much such a change would cost. Officers who work in departmental records may sell confidential information to other officers.

Internal payoffs could involve department's selling positions. At this time, a federal grand jury is reviewing FBI reports concerning allegations that applicants to the Shelby County, Tennessee Sheriff's Department were asked to pay as much as $7,000 to obtain jobs as deputies (*Law Enforcement News,* September 30, 1995, p. 5).

For such transaction as **internal payoffs** to occur, both parties would, in all probability, have to have already been involved in some corrupt practices. In all likelihood, the work assignment would be one with a high corruption potential.

Evidence or records would probably be sold for use in some other pattern of corruption, such as a **shakedown** or **protection of illegal activities.** I feel confident that this is the rarest form of police corruption because police officers are the victims and **internal payoffs** would only occur in departments riddled with the other patterns of corruption.

It is extremely unlikely that all the patterns of corruption identified in this chapter would occur in any one law enforcement agency. I have tried to identify the patterns that could possibly occur. We have to be able to recognize and identify the possible forms of behavior that could occur in order to ensure that they do not occur. Each and every police officer must understand what he or she may come into contact with. This has to be conveyed through formal training and peer group socialization.

Chapter 7
CORRUPT PRACTICES

If we are to understand corrupt behavior, we must recognize that corrupt practices will vary according to organization and officer involvement. Patterns representing adventitious corruption are not organized since they occur opportunistically. Other patterns such as **Protection of Illegal Activities** are often highly organized (see Table 7-1).

Opportunistic events such as "scores" are most often one time events which are never repeated between the same officer and a citizen, victim, or criminal. Other corrupt activities feature a continuing relationship among parties to the corruption. There will be active cooperation among officers. There can also be passive cooperation among officers when "honest" officers do not report their colleagues. There will also be citizen-police cooperation, particularly in vice operations. The length of time that this cooperation takes place will also vary. Obviously, the longer the length of cooperation the more serious the problem.

Corrupt Officers: "Rotten Apples"

The traditional view and the one most often expressed by police executives in the past was that police corruption was the result of a few **rotten apples** in an otherwise honest police department. These **rotten apples** were either weak individuals who had slipped through the screening process and succumbed to the temptations inherent in police work, or they were deviant individuals who continue their deviant practices in an environment of ample opportunity.

Now there is no denying that the very nature of the occupation provides the law enforcement officer with more than ample opportunity to engage in a wide variety of corrupt activities. The police come in contact with a wide variety of deviant actors during their normal work routine, often under conditions of little or no supervision. Simply put, police work is "morally dangerous" work. The nature of police duties, working alone or in pairs beyond the eyes of any immediate supervisor, also presents the officer with situations to engage in other work-related

Table 7-1
PATTERNS OF POLICE CORRUPTION

Pattern	Acts	Organization
Corruption of authority	Free meals, liquor services discounts, rewards	No organization
Kickbacks	Money, goods, and services from those who service clients of the police (garages, bondsman, towing companies, etc.)	Higher, collision
Opportunistic theft	Thefts from arrestees, victims, crime scenes, and unprotected property	None
Shakedowns	Money, goods, or other valuables from criminals or traffic offenders	None
Protection of illegal activities	Protection money from vice operators or companies operating illegally	High; often highly unorganized
The fixes	Quashing of prosecution proceedings or disposal of traffic tickets	Medium; fixers could be on the payroll
Direct criminal activities	Police officers engaged in such crimes as burglary, robbery, etc.	Low; small groups
Internal payoffs	Sale of work assignment, off-days, evidence, and promotions	Low to high; depending on other forms of corruption present

deviance (norm or rule violating behavior) such as brutality, sleeping on duty, drinking on duty, sexual misconduct, etc. These will be discussed further later.

The temptations, coupled with the discretion that the officer can and does exercise, makes police work much more "morally dangerous" than any other occupation. The police officer often has to make a judgement on whether or not a violation of the law has taken place. However, the situations that the police officer encounters and the people involved vary.

In many cases, making an arrest or issuing a citation is either not feasible or not the best action to take. For example, arresting all those publicly intoxicated at some sporting events, such as the Talledega or Winston 500 Mile Road Race or a major league football or baseball game, would be impossible or lead to a riot. Would an officer want to arrest all teenagers having illicit sex in a lovers lane or just ask them to put their clothes on and move along? Would it be appropriate to give a speeding citation to a man driving his wife to the hospital because the baby is coming? Should all those taking chances on the weekly office football pool be arrested for gambling? (If the answer to this last question is yes, then maybe he or she should start at the precinct.)

We could go on and on giving examples of situations in which officers would have to make decisions among various options, including making an arrest or issuing a citation. This is not necessary. We only need to recognize that officers can and do exercise discretion. What we want to ensure is that these discretionary decisions are not influenced by offers of money, goods, services, drugs, or sexual favors.

Now, back to our discussion of "rotten apples." The police corruption scandals of the 1970s and 1980s found little support for this theory. Corruption in city after city was found to be systematic rather than individual behavior. The problem was the barrel and not the apples. The term "rotten apple" came to be seen as a management technique or rationalization used by police executives to explain corrupt behavior in their departments. They were trying to use this label to normalize or distance the police department from one or more publicly identified corrupt police officers. There is no denying that some police executives still use the term "rotten apple" to deny that they have problems in their department. They want the public to believe that a publicly identified "corrupt," or for that matter a "racist," cop is an aberration not a department problem. When they are gone, the problem will go away.

However, many of the writers and researchers on this topic, the present author included, may have gone too far in dismissing "rotten apples" as an explanation of police corrupt behavior. Rotten apples do occur in many police organizations but not all police corruption is the result of behavior by lone officers. A true rotten apple is a corrupt officer in a police department in which corrupt practices are truly exceptional. Collusion or organization among police officers will be rare or nonexistent.

The Knapp Commission, which investigated the New York City corruption scandal in the early 1970s, was the first to recognize two types of officers who could qualify as rotten apples: grass eaters and meat eaters (Knapp Commission, 1973). Grass Eaters are officers who engage in relatively minor types of corruption as the opportunity presents itself. Meat Eaters are police officers who actively seek out corruption opportunities and engage in both minor and major patterns of corruption. Typical patterns engaged in by the **meat eaters** are corruption of authority, kickbacks, opportunistic thefts, shakedowns, fixes, and direct criminal activities. Typically, these patterns do not require a great deal of organization and collusion.

Generally speaking, rotten apples are uncovered internally by fellow police officers. In a truly honest police organization, especially one that has a proactive internal affairs division, corrupt officers will soon be identified. However, this does not mean that all corrupt officers uncovered internally and labeled rotten apples are such.

Corrupt Groups

In some police departments small groups of rotten apples are able to come together and practice their deviant activities. If individual police officers engage in corrupt practices for any length of time without the department discovering it or taking action if they know of it, it is almost inevitable that they will become known to each other and begin to act in collusion. These officers will begin to organize for corrupt activities. However, corrupt practices will not be widespread in the department. That is, not yet.

The typical patterns of corruption practiced by these corrupt groups are direct criminal activities with burglaries, robberies, and drug trafficking as the most common acts. However, small groups can easily engage in kickbacks and protection of illegal activities.

Corrupt groups are also uncovered internally in most instances. Small corrupt groups in a "clean" police department will be rare and short-lived. Nevertheless, many groups of corrupt officers uncovered internally and labeled as such may be officers in "not so clean" departments who have gone beyond the bounds of acceptable behavior and created a scandal.

Corrupt Police Departments

Unfortunately, the worst case scenario has occurred. This is the case where a sizable number, if not the majority, of the police officers in some departments engage in corrupt activities. The most extreme example of a corrupt police department would be a department that adopts corrupt goals. This occurs when the department is "captured" by the political environment or the "dominant coalition" adopts personal gain as a goal (Sherman, 1978:32). The author had the unfortunate experience of working in such a department.

All the patterns of corruption would be found in a corrupt police organization. Those patterns involving vice operations would predominate. Even though a sizable number of the officers would engage in corrupt activities, not all would do so. There are actually five categories of officers who could possibly exist in a corrupt department (Barker, 1986).

Types of Officers in Corrupt Police Organizations

1. White Knights. These officers are honest to a fault or at least they say they are. They often take an extreme position on ethical issues. Although police officers are expected to be ethical and moral in their behavior, white knights can create problems in an organization by being too rigid and judgmental in an occupation that requires discretionary decision making. I was always taught to be wary of anyone that took an extreme position on any issue. Often, those who take extreme positions, and they are usually vocal about it, are trying to convince themselves. Honest and ethical individuals do not have to go around beating on their chests and publicly announcing their virtue. When they do exist in a police department, white knights are in the minority and on a continuum of officers would appear on the extreme left (see below).

Continuum of Officers in Corrupt Departments

White Knights	Straight Shooters	Grass Eaters	Meat Eaters	Rogues

2. Straight Shooters. These are "honest" officers who will overlook the indiscretions of other officers. They do so for pragmatic reasons ("don't make waves," "there is nothing one person can do," "I'm not going to be a snitch," etc.) or for reasons of comradeship ("we have to protect each other," "cops don't turn in other cops," etc.). Not being comfortable with turning in a fellow officer, these officers will accept the fact that other officers engage in some patterns of corruption and misconduct but will not accept others. As one officer related to me, "I never took a bribe and I always refuse gratuities, except for free coffee, for which I always leave a big tip. However, if someone got their head thumped, not 'LA style', but a police rap to get their attention, I didn't see it." Officers in this category in a corrupt police department generally suffer in silence or seek out corruption free assignments.

3. Grass Eaters. As stated previously, these officers engage in some corrupt activities as the occasion and opportunity arises. However, most will have their limits and engage primarily in accepting gratuities, occasional kickbacks, and opportunistic thefts.

4. Meat Eaters. These officers actively seek out opportunities for corruption. They come to work with the idea of making money. They will develop the corruption potential of their beats and assignments.

5. Rogues. The rogue police officer is one who is thoroughly corrupt and considered an aberration even by the **meat eaters.** The rogue will often commit highly visible shakedowns of citizens, felony fixes, and even direct criminal activities. Fortunately, they are a minority even in the most corrupt police organizations. On the continuum of officers, they are on the extreme right and in small numbers.

A recent example of a rogue cop and a "rotten apple" in a department with a reputation for honesty is a Pennsylvania State Police narcotics investigator who was sentenced in 1991 to 17½ years in prison for involvement in a cocaine trafficking ring. He was one of five men convicted of conspiring to sell more than 25 kilograms of cocaine. At the time of his sentencing, the investigator was serving a 5–10 year prison term on a 1989 conviction of involuntary deviate sexual intercourse with a 15-year-old girl (*Law Enforcement News,* November 30, 1991, p. 2).

Generally speaking, corruption in corrupt police organizations is uncovered externally through a scandal. Actions on part of both **white knights** and **rogue officers** have led to scandals. A **white knight** blowing the whistle to the media or an external agency, or the outrageous behavior of a rogue officer cannot be covered up. The investigation and prosecution of police officers in corrupt police departments is usually handled by an outside agency.

Chapter 8

POLICE MISCONDUCT

There are other police ethical violations that do not have a direct link to corruption. Although they do involve the misuse of the officer's official position, they do not involve any material reward or gain. Therefore, police misconduct would be all forms of deviance (norm or rule violating behavior) that does not include a material reward or gain. The most common forms are brutality, sexual misconduct, lying, and the use of drugs. Other forms include sleeping on duty, drinking on duty, and violating departmental rules and regulations.

Police Brutality

Police brutality, like pornography, is in many ways hard to define. Justice Potter Stewart is reported to have said that pornography was hard to define but he knew it when he saw it. Police brutality may also be hard to define, but anyone who has over a year's experience on the street knows it when he/she sees it. I was asked the day after the Rodney King incident if I thought that the actions taken against King were police brutality. I said that I thought they were. Then I was asked if the officers were guilty of assault. I responded that I did not know. I did not know the California statute on assault. My belief that Rodney King was a victim of police brutality was based on my opinion that the force used against him was unreasonable and unnecessary use of force.

Police brutality is the unreasonable and unnecessary use of force. This includes the use of more force than is necessary to effect an arrest or conduct a search. During an arrest, force may occur in four situations. The officer/s may have to use force to effect or complete the arrest. The subject may not actually resist, but he or she may not willingly cooperate either. In the event that the subject resists the arrest, the officer or officers may have to use force to overcome that resistance. On occasion, the officer/s may have to use physical force to maintain the subject in custody or to regain custody should the subject attempt to or escape.

Lastly, officers may legally use force up to and including deadly force to defend themselves or others.

Police brutality also includes the wanton or intentional use of physical force by a police officer. As stated above, unreasonable and unnecessary are ambiguous terms and depend on the circumstances involved. However, any wanton or intentional force used during an arrest situation or while the subject is in custody for the purpose of punishment is unreasonable and unnecessary and therefore, by definition, an act of police brutality.

There are several possible reasons why an officer might engage in an act of brutality. He or she may be the pathological personality who enjoys physically abusing and hurting others. Many experienced police officers have probably come in contact with such individuals in their careers. These violent men (There may be violent women, but I can cite no evidence to support this) are a small minority of the police occupation, but, unfortunately, they do exist. Police departments are well advised to keep good records on resisting and assaulting a police officer arrests along with records of shooting incidents. Violent individuals are soon identified through proactive efforts and should be dealt with as soon as possible. A good psychological evaluation at the initial screening process can usually eliminate most of these individuals.

Some instances of police brutality are the result of fear, with the officer overreacting to what are, or what he or she perceives to be, a dangerous situation. Some of these individuals reacting to cultures or individuals whom they do not understand may believe that physical force is an absolute necessity in the "street jungle." This will be compounded in those departments that hire from the majority and place them in minority settings.

Verbal abuse and provocation can often lead to police brutality. Demonstrators have often tried, and been successful, particularly in the 1960s and 1970s, to provoke officers into the use of force. In the "age of the camcorder," officers have to be aware that film footage of police brutality can help any cause or group. A police officer does not have the legal right to strike an individual who has insulted him or her or called them a profane name, but sometimes the officer may be pushed beyond endurance. Actually, an officer who reacts to such abuse and provocation has compounded his or her problems because now they will have to lie to a supervisor, on a report or even in court to escape disciplinary action.

Police brutality is also used against certain groups and individuals as punishment. The officer may believe that physical force is acceptable under certain circumstances: to command respect, to obtain information, or to punish certain classes of offenders (sex offenders, child molesters, hardened criminals). Often classes of individuals, such as "gang bangers," radicals, hillbillies, "assholes," turds, dirt-bags, etc., are likely to become a victim of brutality.

Those who resist arrest or run from the police in a pursuit are particularly vulnerable targets of police brutality. My research into police pursuits has lead to the conclusion that a high number of injuries to the driver, and sometimes the occupants, occurs when the pursuit has ended and the parties are in custody. Recall that the Rodney King incident started with a pursuit by the California Highway Patrol. These injuries occur, for the most part, because the officer/s are still pumped up with adrenalin and mad. They take their revenge. The author has also been told by numerous officers through the years that any force short of killing the suspect is acceptable whenever an individual resists arrest.

> When someone resists arrest you have to teach him a lesson. You have to. He may kill the next cop who tries to arrest him. My sergeant says there is no resisting unless the man goes to the hospital. So we send them [resisters] to the hospital.

Sex on Duty

Obviously, the male officer comes into contact with a number of females during his routine patrol duties. These contacts often occur under conditions that provide opportunities for illicit sex. The women and the officers are frequently alone and supervision of the officers on patrol is usually minimal. Officers working the late night shifts have the added cover of darkness and little traffic on the road. The officer also has the opportunity to stop women coming from a night of drinking. An intoxicated female may decide that her sexual favors are a small price to pay in order to avoid an arrest for driving while intoxicated.

Allen Sapp (1991) has identified seven categories of police sexually motivated or sexual harassment behaviors.

Nonsexual Contact. This involves behaviors that are sexually motivated without direct sexual actions or inferences. The female citizen may not be aware of the underlying motivations of the officer. However, Sapp says that this behavior is a form of sexual harassment because the officer initiates the contact without legal basis or probable cause. The officer is motivated by a desire to get a closer look at the female or gain information about her. The invalid traffic stop is a good example of this category.

Officers may also stop a female on foot under one pretense or another to obtain information or initiate a conversation. Some of these stops may be followed up by more direct sexual contacts.

Voyeuristic Contact. Some officers spend their time seeking opportunities to view unsuspecting women partially clad or nude. They are literally "peeping Toms" in uniform. The most common form of this category of behavior are officers who seek out parked cars in "lovers lanes" hoping to observe sexual activities. They sometimes park their cars and "sneak" up on the occupants.

Contacts With Crime Victims. Sapp says that female victims of crime are particularly susceptible to sexual harassment by police officers. They are vulnerable because they are often emotionally upset and turn to the police for support and assistance. Unnecessary callbacks to the residence of the female are one of the most common forms of this behavior. The officer's frequent trips to female victim's residence are for the purpose of initiating some sexual contact.

Sex crimes victims are also susceptible to sexual harassment by police officers. Some of this is unintentional when it results from a lack of sensitivity and knowledge on the officer's part. However, when an officer questions the victim beyond the depth of details needed for investigation purposes, this is sexual harassment.

Contacts With Offenders. Female offenders are in a vulnerable position when it comes to being a victim of sexual harassment or sexual contact. They are aware of the authority of the officer and that their complaints may be disregarded or played down. They are subject to sexual demands or body searches, frisks, or pat downs.

Contacts With Juvenile Offenders. On occasion, police officers have sexually harassed or had sexual contacts with runaways, truants, and delinquents. Sapp believes that this is the rarest form of sexual misconduct by police officers. I hope he is right.

Sexual Shakedowns. In this category, police officers demand sexual services from prostitutes or other citizens involved in illegal or illicit activities. These are sexual activities involving an unwilling victim who yields solely on the basis of the police authority to arrest and prosecute. Rape is the correct term for this behavior.

Citizen-Initiated Sexual Contacts. Some sexual contacts are initiated by the female citizen and not the officers. Most police departments have stories about "police groupies" who are attracted to uniforms, weapons, or the authority of the police. Police officers also get calls from lonely or mentally disturbed women who want attention or affection. Some women will commit minor traffic violations as a ruse to see if the officer is interested in sexual contact. Women also seek sexual contact in return for favors, preferential treatment, or additional protection. Obviously, women working in certain illegal occupations such as prostitutes or pornographers have a great deal to gain from a good working relationship with the police.

Sleeping On Duty

Sleeping while at work probably occurs in all occupations where workers engage in late-night shift work under minimal supervision, such as night watchman, factory workers, and the military. However, this form of misconduct may be especially prevalent among police officers on the last shift. The police patrol car is sometimes referred to as a "traveling bedroom" because of the amount of sleeping and sex that takes place in it. The terms "hole" and "coop" are familiar to most police officers.

The nature of the job has some influence on the amount of sleeping that takes place. The most obvious influence is the fact that police operations take place 24 hours a day and the rest of society operates for the most part during daylight hours. Therefore, it takes a great deal of adjustment on the part of night workers, particularly cops, to accomplish what are routine day activities for others. Oftentimes, the criminal justice system also creates problems. The night working officer's court appearances are scheduled during the day. This often results in the officer spending his/her entire day in court following a tour of duty and then having to return to duty the same night. In addition, night tours are often extremely dull and monotonous with usually only security checks to perform. When lack of sleep during the day and dull and monotonous duties at night are combined with minimal, nonexistent, or poor supervision, a certain amount of sleeping becomes inviting.

Off-duty activities may also force the officer to catch up on his/her sleep. The officer who moonlights during the day soon finds it hard to stay awake at night. Many officers who attend college during the day either study or sleep during their shift. Finally, some officers sleep in their cars for the same reason that clerks sleep in their stockroom; they are alienated with their job.

Drinking on Duty

Drinking on duty is a serious form of police misconduct. The officer who drinks on the job presents a grave threat to citizens and his/her fellow officers. He or she is armed and usually in command of a powerful police vehicle. Mistakes made by an intoxicated police officer can cause serious injuries and even death to citizens and other police officers.

Drinking on duty, as with sleeping on duty, can also be a symptom of alienation from the job. It may also be the result of boredom, monotony, and opportunity combined with ineffectual supervision. Alcoholism among police officers can be a serious problem because of the endless opportunities they have to drink while on duty.

Use of Drugs

The abuse of drugs, other than alcohol, by law enforcement officers has received a great deal of attention. However, Carter and Stephens (1991) arrived at two conclusions based on their research in this area: (1) a strong impression that incidents of police corruption associated with drug trafficking either by law enforcement officers or through the assistance of police is increasing [I would certainly agree with this] and (2) some police officers use drugs as a recreational activity. I have already discussed the relationship between corruption and drugs. Therefore, I will confine my remarks to the use of drugs as misconduct not related to corruption.

Police officers often come from a population group where the use of drugs was prevalent and they have been exposed to their use as recreation. In fact, some officers have been occasional and recreational users of drugs prior to joining the force. Some might accept and agree with the rationalizations offered for off-duty drug use, particularly if the drugs are in the "less dangerous" categories, i.e., not crack, cocaine, LSD, heroin, or speed. However, one must face the fact that such use is against the law, unethical, and forbidden by police departments' rules and regulations. One must also acknowledge that even in population groups where occasional use does take place, not all engage in this behavior. There is also the danger that recreational use can lead to instances of police corruption and drug use on duty.

Police Lying

Police officers lie to citizens, each other, suspects, victims, the media, in court, and to other criminal justice officials. In fact, one can say that lying and other deceptive practices are an integral part of the police officer's working environment (Barker and Carter, 1991). These lies and deceptive practices vary as to whether or not they should be considered ethical violations or are necessary for the police to accomplish their tasks.

Accepted Lies. Lies in this category are those considered to be an accepted part of an officer's working environment. They are told because they fulfill a defined law enforcement mission. The police organization and its members will freely admit that they are engaging in deceptive practices. The most obvious example of accepted lying are the lies and deceptive practices engaged in by undercover officers. Secret and consensual crime operations could probably not be carried out without some deceptive practices. Police officers engaged in these activities must not only conceal their true identity but they must talk, act, and dress out of character. They must fabricate all kinds of stories to perform these duties. One can hardly imagine that FBI Special Agent Joseph Pistone could have operated for six years in the Mafia without the numerous number of lies he had to tell (Pistone, 1987). He was so successful that he was asked to become a "made" member of the Mafia before he was withdrawn.

The overwhelming majority of undercover operations are neither as fascinating nor as dangerous as working six years with the Mafia or some other organized crime group. The most common operations occur in routine vice operations dealing with prostitution, bootlegging, gambling, narcotics, bribery of public officials (e.g., ABSCAM, MILAB, BRILAB) and sting operations.

However, this area is not without its problems. Marx (1985) has pointed out that sometimes these practices can lead to a situation in which the police go beyond determining if a suspect is breaking the law and attempt to see if the person can be induced into breaking the law. This sort of activity raises the specter of entrapment. The "Dirty Harry" problem in police work, where some officers believe that the end justifies the means, raises the question as to what extent morally good police practices warrant or justify ethically, politically, or legally suspect means to achieve law enforcement activities (Klockers, 1980).

Encouraging the commission of a crime may be a legally accepted police practice when the officer acts as a willing victim or his or her actions facilitate the commission of a crime which was going to be committed in the first place. However, it is possible for "encouragement" to lead the suspect to raise the defense of entrapment. According to *Black's Law Dictionary,* entrapment is "the act of officers or agents of the government inducing a person to commit a crime not contemplated by him, for the purpose of instituting a criminal prosecution against him (277)." In order for the defense of entrapment to prevail, the defendant must show that the officer or his/her agent (informant in most cases) has gone beyond providing the encouragement and opportunity for the commission of a crime and through trickery, fraud, or other deception has induced the suspect to commit a crime. This defense is raised far more times than it is successful because the current legal criteria to determine entrapment is what is known as the "subjective test."

In the "subjective test," the predisposition of the offender, rather than the objective methods of the law enforcement officer, is the key to determining entrapment (Skolnick, 1982, Marx, 1985, Stitt and James, 1985). This test makes it extremely difficult for a defendant with a criminal record to claim that he/she would not have committed the crime except for the action of the officer. Another test the "objective test" raised by a minority of the Supreme Court has focused on the nature of the law enforcement officer's conduct rather than the predisposition of the offender (Stitt and James, 1985). For example, the "objective test" probably would examine whether the production of crack cocaine by a police organization for use in undercover drug arrests is proper and legal. According to an Associated Press story, the Broward County Florida Sheriff's Department, not having enough crack to supply undercover officers, manufactured its own crack. The sheriff's department chemist made at least $20,000 worth of the illegal substance. Local defense attorneys raised the issue of entrapment. One public defender stated:

> I think there's something sick about this whole system where the police make the product, sell the product and arrest people for buying the product (*Birmingham Post Herald,* April 19, 1989:B2).

What do you think? In my opinion, deceptive practices aside, having a law enforcement agent make an illegal drug and then sell it to others and then arrest those who buy it does raise a number of ethical and legal issues. At what point do we draw the line to make a police undercover operation convincing? Fortunately, the practice cited above was stopped as soon as the media got wind of it. The current "war on drugs" is raising many issues in this area. Black-clad police "Ninja Warriors" have been accused of violating citizens' civil rights as they stage "whoops raids" (wrong person or address), use unreliable and nonexistent informers and overly destructive search techniques in the war. There have been several successful civil suits that have awarded damages to complainants for police overzealousness in this area. The police must be careful that the ends do not become more important than the means of accomplishing them. "Dirty Harry" may be a character we applaud on the screen, but we shouldn't want him or anyone like him working for our police department.

In addition to the accepted practices of lying, required for undercover operations, members of the police community often believe that it is proper to lie to the media or the public when it is necessary to protect the innocent, protect the image of the department, or calm the public in a crisis situation. The department's official policy may be one of openness and candor when dealing with the media. However, as a practical matter, members of the department may deny the existence of an investigation or "plant" erroneous information (i.e., disinformation) to protect an ongoing investigation. The untimely revelation of facts may alert the suspects and drive them underground or cause them to cease their illegal activities. Nevertheless, one could argue that public exposure of certain criminal activities or the possibility of them might decrease the risk of injury to persons or property. This issue was raised in the terrorist bombing of Pan Am flight 103 over Lockerbie, Scotland. What was the best course of action? Tell the public of all threats against airliners—most of which are unfounded—and create fear, or keep all threats confidential and hope that airline and government officials effectively deal with the threats. Since Lockerbie, the law enforcement posture, at least at the national level, seems to be to tell the public of all threats.

In 1991, the residents of Buffalo, New York's depressed east side were angry at their police department for waiting months to reveal that a serial rapist was attacking young girls on their way to school. A total of 11 girls between the ages of 9 and 16 were raped. After the third rape the police had determined that a serial rapist was at work, but they held off telling residents for fear that sensationalized news coverage would hinder their investigation (*Law Enforcement News,* April 30, 1991, p. 2). What should the police have done? What is more important—the possibility of keeping young girls from being raped or a successful investigation? Is it moral or ethical to keep such information from the public? You be the judge.

We must recognize that in some crimes, such as kidnapping, the publication of any information at all might lead to the murder of the victim. Therefore, under these circumstances, law enforcement officials or officers might view lies told to protect the victim as perfectly acceptable and necessary.

Police administrators are also aware that the entire organization may be labeled corrupt because of the corrupt acts of some of its members. The "rotten apple" theory of police corruption mentioned earlier was viewed as an "acceptable lie" to prevent this. Thus accepted lies are those which the organization and its members view as having a viable role in police operations. The criteria for the lie to be accepted are:

> It must be in furtherance of a legitimate organizational purpose.
>
> There must be a clear relationship between the need to deceive and the accomplishment of an organizational purpose.
>
> The nature of the deception must be one wherein officers and the management structure acknowledge that deception will better serve the public interest than the truth.
>
> The ethical standing of the deception and the issue of law appears to be a collateral concern.

Tolerated Lying. Tolerated lies are those recognized as lies by the police organization but tolerated as "necessary evils." They are situational or "white" lies told when it is not possible to explain the truth. For example, police officials will often claim to practice full enforcement of all laws at all times rather than try to explain police discretionary decisions. At the scene of a crime, an officer may lie to a victim rather than reveal that there is no chance to catch the perpetrator or recover stolen property.

As one can imagine, the interrogation stage of an arrest is an area filled with tolerated lying. According to many police officers and textbooks on the subject, telling the subject that there is evidence to link him/her to the crime or that fellow subjects have confessed are "good" interrogation techniques. One could say that the means justifies the ends. However, lies told under these circumstances could and have lead innocent persons to succumb to the powerful persuasion of a police officer and admit to crimes they did not commit.

Deviant Lying. This third category of police lying has two forms. **Deviant lying** involves lies that violate substantive or procedural laws and police department rules and regulations.

Deviant Lies in Support of Perceived Legitimate Goals. The deviant lies told by law enforcement officers to achieve perceived legitimate goals usually occur to put criminals in jail, prevent crime, and perform other policing responsibilities. The law enforcement officer may feel that because of his/her unique experiences in dealing with criminals and the public that they intuitively know the guilt or innocence of those they arrest. They will feel this way independently of any legal standards. However, the final determination of guilt is in the judicial process. The officer/s convinced that the suspect is factually guilty of the offense may believe that the necessary elements of legal guilt may be missing, e.g., no probable cause for a stop, no **Miranda** warning, not enough narcotics for a felony offense, etc. Therefore, the officer feels that he or she must supply the missing elements to prevent a guilty person from walking. One police officer told me that it was often necessary to "fluff up the evidence" to get a search warrant or insure a conviction. The officer will attest to facts, statements, or evidence which never occurred or occurred in a different fashion. Obviously, when he/she does this under oath, perjury has been committed.

Once a matter of record, the perjury must continue for the officer to avoid facing disciplinary action and even criminal prosecution. Whether or not this occurred in the O.J. Simpson trial is still a matter of debate. However, the evidence is overwhelming that at least one police officer lied in that case. Unfortunately, this trial has introduced a new term into the discussion of police testimony—**testilying.** We may not like this term and all it implies, but we are going to have to deal with it and insure that **testilying** does not occur.

Evidence of **testilying** did not first appear in the Simpson trial. In 1989, charges were dropped in a case against a cop killer and three Boston police officers were suspended with pay pending a perjury investigation. The perjury involved a Boston detective who "invented" an informant. The detective maintained that the informant gave the critical information which was cited in the affidavit for a search warrant (*New York Times*, 1989:K9). The "no knock" search warrant's execution led to the death of a Boston detective. In 1991, the Boston detective who "invented" the informant was sentenced to five years probation for perjury (*Law Enforcement News,* June 15/30, 1991, p. 2).

Similarly, the officer who lies in these instances must employ creative writing skills on official reports to ensure that the written chronology of events is consistent with criminal procedures, regardless of what actually occurred. As I have often stated in the police academy, the problem with lies is that the truth has instant recall; lies don't. If you tell a lie, especially in a criminal case, you are going to have to constantly recall what was written on the official report, what was told to the sergeant, to Internal Affairs, on the stand, etc. Sooner or later it may all come unraveled as it did with Mark Furhman.

Deviant Lies in Support of Illegitimate Goals. Lies in this category are told to effect an act of corruption or to protect an officer from organizational discipline or civil and/or criminal liability. The officer who commits perjury in court may do so to "fix" a criminal prosecution for monetary reward. In fact, lying and/or perjury in court or before other criminal justice officials is an absolute necessity in departments where corrupt acts occur on a routine basis. Sooner or later every police officer who engages in corrupt acts or observes fellow officers engaging in corrupt acts will face the possibility of having to lie under oath to protect himself/herself or fellow officers.

There is always the distinct possibility that engaging in other forms of police misconduct will lead to deviant lying. To avoid the possibility of criminal and/or civil liability, the officer who engages in an act of brutality will have to lie on an official report, to his or her supervisor, and possibly during testimony. The officer who engages in a police action (pursuit, use of force, etc.) that is against the department's policy and results in death or injury may have to lie or perjure himself to protect himself or fellow officers.

Chapter 9

CONTROL OF CORRUPTION AND MISCONDUCT

The last question to be asked is: Can police corruption and misconduct be controlled? You notice that I did not ask if it can be eliminated. Police corruption and misconduct can never be entirely eliminated from any police organization. That is an unrealistic expectation. Just as a society without crime will never exist, a police organization where no corruption or misconduct occurs will never exist. However, both corruption and misconduct can be controlled and managed by a three-pronged effort directed toward (1) decreasing the opportunity; (2) undermining group support for corruption; and (3) increasing the risk.

Decreasing the Opportunity

Stance of the Administrator

The police chief executive must convey his posture on corruption and serious misconduct issues such as brutality and lying to the department and the public. This is especially true for those administrators who have been hired as change agents after a public scandal. If corruption has been a problem in the past, the new CEO must recognize that it has and inform the officers that the practices will end. Of course, the new chief is not in the position to grant general amnesty for past events, especially those which involved serious criminal violations. However, the new law enforcement executive officer can set the tone for the agency by developing an anticorruption and antimisconduct policy with its attendant rules and procedures. The department's policy will set the limits for all members of the organization.

A Note on Policy Development

Policy is defined as the principles and values which guide the performance of a departmental activity. These principles and values are "attitude forming" in the sense that they tell departmental personnel how to think about performing their duties (Hoy, 1982: 301). A policy is *not* a statement of what must be done in a particular situation. It is a statement of guiding principles which should be followed in order to attain some departmental goal or objective. Policy should always be thought of as the framework for drafting procedures and rules and regulations.

EXAMPLES

CORRUPTION

1. PURPOSE

The purpose of this policy is to prevent corruption from occurring in this law enforcement agency and to prescribe actions to be taken in the event that corruption is alleged and/or identified.

2. POLICY

It is the policy of this law enforcement agency to establish proactive procedures to prevent corruption and to investigate and prosecute corruption to the full extent of the law, and administrative authority, when reported or identified (IACP Model Policy, 1989).

MISCONDUCT

1. PURPOSE

The purpose of this policy is to provide all sworn employees with notice of the provisions of the department's drug-testing program.

2. POLICY

It is the policy of this department that the critical mission of law enforcement justifies maintenance of a drug-free work environment through the use of a reasonable employee drug-testing program.

The law enforcement profession has several uniquely compelling interests that justify the use of employee drug-testing. The public has a right to expect that those who are sworn to protect them are at all times both physically and mentally prepared to assume these duties. There is sufficient evidence to conclude that the use of controlled substances, and other forms of drug abuse will seriously impair an employee's physical and mental health, and thus job performance.

Where law enforcement officers participate in illegal drug use and drug activity, the integrity of the law enforcement profession, and public confidence in it are destroyed. This confidence is further eroded by the potential for corruption created by drug use.

Therefore, in order to ensure the integrity of the department, and to preserve public trust and confidence in a fit and drug-free law enforcement profession, this department shall implement a drug-testing program to detect drug use by sworn officers.

As one can see from the examples, policy can be very broad and allow some flexibility and it is subject to varying interpretations. Therefore, the agency must define the terms and limit the flexibility and discretion through procedures, rules, and regulations.

Procedures are the methods of performing an operation or the manner in which the task is to be performed. Procedures are different from policy in that they direct the action to be taken within policy guidelines. Policy and procedures are both objective-oriented; however, policy establishes limits of action while procedures direct responses within these limits (Carter & Dearth, 1984). Procedures allow for some flexibility within limits and they are usually found in instructional materials and manuals as well as in policy statements. For clarification purposes, we will provide procedures for the policies on Corruption Prevention and Drug testing outlined above.

EXAMPLES

CORRUPTION

IV. PROCEDURES

2. Code of Ethics

This department will maintain, periodically review and update a Code of Ethics.

Each new employee will be required to read and place his/her signature at the bottom of a copy of the Code of Ethics as an indicator that he/she has read and understands the standards of conduct set forth in the Code of Ethics.

3. Rules of Conduct (R.O.C.):

The Rules of Conduct shall appear in front of the policy manual to emphasize their significance. New employees will be instructed in the R.O.C. The R.O.C. will be reviewed annually for relevance, timeliness, adequacy and completeness.

MISCONDUCT

IV. PROCEDURES
F. DRUG-TESTING METHODOLOGY

1. The testing or processing phase shall consist of a two-step procedure:
    a. Initial screening test, and
    b. Confirmation test.

Rules and **regulations** are actually synonymous and refer to specific requirements or prohibitions which prevent deviations from policies or procedures. A violation or a rule/regulation usually invites disciplinary action. If policies are "attitude forming" and guide judgements, rules are "behavior forming" and govern behavior. Rules are restrictive and allow for no flexibility or discretionary behavior. They should only be used when absolutely necessary to ensure compliance with some desired behavior or action. Unfortunately, some police administrators confuse rules with policy and procedures and believe the only way to control behavior is through a proliferation of rules and regulations. This is self-defeating because the proliferation of rules and regulations creates an illusion of control yet not genuine control (Cordner, 1989). This simple solution ignores the purpose of policy development and the effects of training, education and good supervision.

Even though too many rules may be counterproductive, there are instances where police behavior or misbehavior must be prevented. In these instances, rules are necessary.

EXAMPLES

CORRUPTION

Narcotics and/or Drug Enforcement:
   a) Two or more officers must be present to effect any arrests resulting from a planned drug operation.
   b) All confidential informants and drug buys will conform to control, bookkeeping, and accountability procedures.
   c) All evidence will be processed strictly according to the policies and procedures governing the property and evidence functions.

MISCONDUCT

A. Prohibited Activity

The following rules shall apply to all applicants, probationary and sworn employees, while on and off duty:

1. No employee shall illegally possess any controlled substance.
2. No employee shall ingest any controlled or other dangerous substance, unless as prescribed by a licensed medical practitioner.

In addition to writing realistic and meaningful policies, procedures, and rules, the law enforcement executive must also ensure that his or her public statements on the subject of corruption are not unrealistic and pompous. Telling the press and the troops that "Police officers in my department arrest everyone who breaks the law. There will be no opportunities for corruption," "Corruption starts with a free cup of coffee," "There will be no fat cops eating apples in this department," will be viewed with skepticism and disgust. Police behavior should be guided and directed by realistic expectations. If you don't mean it, don't say it.

It should go without saying that the law enforcement executive's behavior should conform to his/her public pronouncements and the department's policies, procedures, and rules. However, this is not always the case. There have been several recent well publicized examples where the attitude has been "do as I say, not as I do." A chief accepting free rooms and meals, even though out of his home city, because of his position, raises ethical issues and invites criticism.

Educating the Public

As part of his/her efforts to decrease the opportunities for corruption, the chief executive officer must educate the public concerning their efforts in corruption control. He/she may have to make public appearances before civic and professional groups where restaurant owners, barkeepers, construction firms, etc., are present and explain the department's policy on gifts and other gratuities. At first, he/she may face some opposition and the comment that "it is my business and I will do what I want." However, once they understand that it is department policy for its officers not to accept the offered gifts and gratuities, things should straighten themselves out. They should be informed of the risk they are creating for the officer should he/she accept the gift or gratuity. They should also be encouraged to report any solicitations by police officers.

Increased Supervision

In today's world, police officers, often totally alone and unobserved, may be placed in a position where the money from a bribe or drug shakedown opportunity may be more than an entire year's salary. Corruption thrives best in poorly-run organizations where lines of authority are vague and supervision is minimal (Goldstein, 1975:42). Increased supervision can somewhat eliminate the opportunity for this to happen. Increased supervision means more than putting more sergeants or lieutenants on the shifts or in the precincts.

Additional supervision means giving police managers the authority and responsibility for anticorruption efforts. Supervisors must understand that they have the primary responsibility for identifying, eliminating, and controlling corruption and misconduct. They should be trained in the techniques, investigative approaches, and procedures to carry-out their responsibilities. Top and middle managers must be held strictly accountable for corruption and misconduct that occurs in their areas of responsibility.

Sustained Action and Monitoring of Legal and Illegal Corruption Hazards

The story is often told of sociologists spending enormous amounts of money researching for vice activities when a hundred dollars to an experienced cab driver would get the same information. Sometimes we wonder why police administrators at the top and middle management could not identify corrupt activities in their commands. There are certain activities and businesses that are natural corruption hazards and indicators of possible police citizen collusion. These must be closely monitored to decrease the opportunity for corruption. In 1979, Ward and McCormack in *An Anti-Corruption Manual for Administrators in Law Enforcement* listed numerous corruption hazards and indicators. Their list is still valuable today. A partial listing follows:

BARS, GRILLS, CABARETS AND BOTTLE CLUBS

Hazard:
> The acceptance of money gifts, free food and drinks by members of the department from owners and operators of bars and grills, cabarets and bottle clubs to overlook violations of the Alcoholic Beverage Control Law, the Health Code, Traffic Regulations and Administrative Code.

Indicators of the Problem

Unexplained visits by department members to bars, grills, cabarets, and other licensed and unlicensed premises, indicated by:

- failure to notify the radio dispatcher of visit.
- failure to notify supervisor on patrol.
- no arrests, summonses, or other police action taken when necessary, and failure to make proper reports.
- improper or incomplete investigations of crimes occurring on or near premises.
- a specific pattern of visits to the premises by members on and off duty.
- the presence of illegal parking in the vicinity without proper police action being taken.

Numerous complaints from the public alleging:

- disorderly premises.
- overcharging for meals, drinks and services.
- adulterated liquor and wine.
- credit cards lost or stolen from clothing checked in cloak rooms or from individuals on the premises.
- police cashing personal checks that subsequently are returned to the bank due to insufficient funds.
- assaults on patrons by employees or persons on the premises.
- improper or no police action taken when police are summoned with complaint to premises for cause.
- taxicab drivers, hotel employees, and others bringing people to prearranged specific locations like bars, clubs and hotels for a fee.
- unlicensed premises (bottle clubs) selling alcoholic beverages.
- premises frequented by persons who are obviously narcotic addicts or prostitutes.
- without appropriate police action subsequently taken, individuals being injured in the vicinity of licensed premises under circumstances that might indicate that the injury occurred within the premises.
- receipt of written or verbal communications alleging an improper presence of police in the premises or alleging some police corruption.
- business being conducted during prohibited hours.
- through personal observations, premises are frequented by known gamblers or racketeers without intelligence reports having been received from patrol service units.

Follow-up inspections reveal that complaints, referred to other commands for action, are not being acted upon effectively.

Inspection of records reveals that cases resulting in arrests or summonses have an inordinately low conviction rate for some premises.

Procedures for Control

"Routine" visits prohibited. Inspections should be conducted on a directed basis by the precinct commanding officer.

Commanding officer or executive officer should direct superior officers to make frequent observations of suspected premises and persons suspected of corrupt practices.

Information received from within the department and the public should be verified.

Conduct personal interview of complainants, when deemed necessary.

Personally inspect and analyze department records to detect possible trends or patterns of police action in connection with premises under suspicion.

Carefully observe members of the department suspected of having a drinking problem that would cause them to become amenable to corruptive efforts by others.

CONSTRUCTION SITES

Hazard

The acceptance or solicitation of money, gifts and building materials by police to overlook violations of the law pertaining to the regulation of construction.

Indicators of Problem

- unexplained visits to construction sites by police while on and off duty.
- police observed placing building materials into department vehicles or into their private vehicles.
- identifiable violations which create safety hazards for pedestrians or which impede traffic flow at construction sites apparently being overlooked by police.
- written or verbal complaints received from the public alleging violations at construction sites without proper police action being taken.
- complaints received from construction workers or site managers alleging excessive enforcement.
- unusual summons activity by a member of the department, followed by sudden inactivity.

Procedures for Control

Direct written or verbal communications to site managers informing them of departmental policy and requesting their cooperation in enforcement. Advise them that the offer of a gratuity to a public officer is a crime and that the person making the offer is subject to arrest. Superior officers should make frequent observations of sites to insure adequate enforcement of pertinent laws and to observe the conduct of police observed at construction sites without sufficient reason for their presence.

Carefully examine summons and other records to detect signs of pressuring site managers by department managers.

Inspect construction sites immediately upon receipt of complaints.

HOTELS AND RESTAURANTS

Hazards

The acceptance of free meals, free rooms, and Christmas gratuities from owners and operators of hotels and restaurants to overlook parking, health codes, administrative code violations, and laws pertaining to public morals.

Police unofficially assisting owners and operators of these premises in maintaining order.

Indicators of Problem

- unexplained visits to the premises by police on duty and off duty.
- receipt of written or oral complaints alleging members are obtaining free meals and rooms.
- observations of violations of laws inside and in the vicinity of the hotels and restaurants without adequate enforcement activity for correction.
- complaints from the public alleging violations of the liquor laws and the laws pertaining to gambling and prostitution that should have been discovered and reported by members of the department.
- complaints, especially those alleging improper police action, of assaults on the public by employees of hotels and restaurants.
- hotels and restaurants having a known policy of free meals, rooms, etc., for "man on post."

Procedures for Control

Make independent observations of premises for an evaluation of any crime problems that may exist.

Direct observations to detect the furnishing of unwarranted police service.

Carefully examine reports on injured individuals and complaint reports, the origins of which may have been in a hotel or restaurant instead of the location where actually reported taking place.

Compare the findings revealed by observations of suspected premises with arrest reports and with the results of other completed investigations.

Disseminate current departmental policy to members and to the owners, managers, and employees of hotels and restaurants and request their cooperation. They should be advised that an offer of a gratuity is a crime and that the person making the offer is subject to arrest.

Provide adequate sleeping facilities in the station house for police who need these facilities.

PARKING LOTS

Hazard

The acceptance by police of money, gifts, free parking privileges, and Christmas gratuities from the owners and operators of parking lots to overlook violations pertaining to their businesses.

Indicators of Problem

- violations of traffic regulations and congested, vehicular traffic in the vicinity of the entrances to parking lots.
- parking of customers' automobiles on streets in violation of departmental regulations.
- deliberate inattention to violations by members on patrol.
- unexplained visits to the parking lots by police while on and off duty.
- written or verbal communications received alleging that police frequently observed overlooking violations.
- complaints from parking lot owners and employees that they are unnecessarily receiving summonses for borderline violations.

Procedures for Control

Observe and inspect patrol supervisors to observe that laws concerning parking lots are being enforced fairly.

Inspect daily activity reports to detect unusual and suspicious trends of activity.

Frequent observations of persons and places susceptible to corruption efforts.

REPAIR SHOPS, GARAGES, TRUCKING COMPANIES

Hazard

The acceptance by police of money, gifts, and free services from owners and operators of repair shops, garages, trucking companies, and vehicle rental companies to overlook violations of the law pertaining to traffic regulations and to general business laws.

Indicators of Problem

- double parking and parking on sidewalks in the vicinity of said businesses, without proper police action being taken.
- loading or unloading in non-loading zones resulting in the obstruction of sidewalks.

- streets or sidewalks being used as storage areas.
- major repairs, other than emergency repairs being performed in the streets.
- receipt of numerous complaints about noise of trucks and cars, without any corrective action taken by patrol service units.
- written and oral communications received from the public alleging collusion between members of the command and the business.
- unexplained visits by members of the command on or off duty to the businesses.
- an inordinate number of rented automobiles recovered through arrests or recovered as abandoned, by specific members of the command. Arrest records could indicate a desire for rewards from the companies.
- complaints received from operators and owners of the businesses, alleging excessive harassment by members of the command.

Procedures for Control

Direct superior officers to observe and inspect businesses frequently to ascertain that traffic regulations and general business laws are being properly enforced. Inspect departmental records to discern possible trends like a lack of summons activity.

GYPSY OR UNLICENSED CABS

Hazard

The acceptance or solicitation by police of money and gifts from gypsy cab drivers and operators of livery car services to overlook violations of traffic regulations.

Indicators of Problem

- stopping an inordinate number of gypsy cabs without arrests being made, summonses being served, or adequate reporting made by members of the command.
- the receipt of a number of written or verbal communications from gypsy cab operators alleging harassment by members of the command.
- rumors circulating within the command concerning the acceptance of bribes from gypsy cab operators, especially if they are related to specific members of the command.
- unexplained visits by police on and off duty to gypsy cab offices or garages.
- failure by patrol services to take corrective action concerning traffic conditions and unnecessary noise in the vicinity of gypsy cab offices and garages.

Procedures for Control

Direct superior officers to observe and to supervise closely members of the command in the enforcement of regulations governing gypsy cabs.

TRAFFIC VIOLATIONS

Hazards

The acceptance or solicitation by police of money and gifts to overlook traffic violations.

Indicators of Problem

- excessive stopping of motorists by police without comparable summons or arrest activity.
- serious traffic and safety conditions—illegal parking, street repairing of automobiles, sidewalk parking, and low enforcement activity—left uncorrected by department members.
- written and verbal complaints received from the public alleging non-enforcement of traffic regulations or alleging payment to police for special treatment.
- receipt of complaints alleging police officers attempted to extort money to overlook violations.

Procedures for Control

Direct superior officers to observe places and persons in areas of traffic to insure adequate enforcement and to prevent corruptive practices.

Closely supervise members assigned to traffic control or parking enforcement duties.

Frequently inspect activity reports to discover possible corruptive practices.

TOW TRUCKS

Hazard

The acceptance or solicitation of money, gifts, and free services by members of the department to overlook violations of the laws governing tow trucks and to compensate police for referring operators of vehicles in accidents to specific companies.

Indicators of Problem

- an inordinate percentage of towing business being handled by a very few towing companies.
- tow truck operators violating traffic regulations without corrective action being taken by patrol officers.

- verbal or written complaints, received from the public alleging collusion between members of the command and tow truck operators.
- members of the command observed in possession of business cards of towing or body-and-fender repair companies.
- the receipt of a substantial number of written and verbal communications from tow truck operators alleging harassment by members of command.

Procedures for Control

Superior officers on patrol should respond to the scene of all accidents requiring tow service.

Direct superior officers to frequently observe suspicious towing operations and suspected department members.

Initiate follow-up investigations of selected collisions involving a tow to determine any possible police corruption.

Distribute to motorists at accident scenes handout sheets describing laws pertaining to tows.

PROSTITUTION

Hazard

The acceptance and solicitation of money and favors by police from prostitutes to overlook violations of the laws relating to prostitution and prostitution-related offenses.

Indicators of Problem

- unnecessary familiarity with known prostitutes while on and off duty.
- failure of the uniformed patrol service to adequately control public nuisance conditions when prostitutes or pimps congregate on streets to actively solicit patrons or when hotels, massage parlors, bars, and apartments are apparently being used by prostitutes.
- the presence, on or off duty, of a member of the command not on police business, at locations frequented by known prostitutes.
- recurring arrests of the same prostitutes as a harassment technique by individual officers for reasons other than impartial law enforcement.
- written and verbal complaints from the public alleging collusion between members of the command and prostitutes.

Procedures for Control

Observe frequently suspicious areas of prostitution, pimps, prostitutes, and police to determine if any corruption patterns exist.

Initiate follow-up inspections to determine what action has been taken by plainclothes units regarding information supplied to them by patrol officers.

GAMBLING

Hazard

The acceptance of solicitation of money and gifts by members of the department from individuals involved in illegal gambling activities to overlook violations of laws regulating gambling.

Indicators of Problem

- known gambling locations operating within the confines of the precinct without proper intelligence reports being submitted by members of the command.
- crowded parking conditions in the vicinity of suspected premises, especially during evening hours, that indicate possible organized card or dice games.
- large numbers of people entering a business establishment like a candy store, shoe shine parlor, or grocery store and leaving without having made a purchase.
- numerous observations of known gamblers at specific locations.
- members of the command, while on or off duty, in the company of known gamblers or frequenting locations suspected of gambling activity.
- failure by patrol officers to correct public nuisance relating to gambling.
- the receipt of written and oral communications alleging that members of the command are permitting gambling to take place.

Procedures for Control

Initiate frequent observations of individuals, locations, and members of the command suspected of being involved in corruption relating to gambling.

Direct superior officers to observe suspicious gambling locations frequently. Initiate follow-up inspections by the commanding officer to determine whether intelligence reports are being submitted for all suspected locations and persons within the command.

NARCOTICS

Hazard

- prior to booking, the unlawful release of prisoners in exchange for money, narcotics, or other gifts.
- unwarranted dismissal of court cases after police conspiracy with offenders.
- the withholding of contraband by police for private use, future sale, or the practice commonly known as "flaking" or placing evidence of a crime on a person who does not actually possess it.

Indicators of Problem

- an arrest pattern by specific officers which indicates a concentration of arrests for loitering and narcotics trafficking by people waiting to buy or sell.
- repeated observations of police at locations frequented by narcotics users, especially when no other police business is occurring at those locations.
- despite the receipt of complaints, narcotic locations flourishing without proper police action being taken.
- a pattern of complaints by prisoners alleging that money, other valuables, and narcotics are missing after the suspects have been searched by police.
- a pattern of complaints that charge improper search and seizure.
- a pattern of allegations of evidence being placed on a supposedly innocent person to justify an arrest.
- an unusual number of court cases being dismissed because of incomplete or faulty court affidavits, poor testimony, or non-appearance of specific members of the department.
- members of the department spending money presumably in excess of their income.
- possible narcotics use by members indicated, in addition to the usual physical signs, by excessive requests for emergency leave; excessive sick report time (noting type of illness), neglect of personal appearance; constant fatigue; inadequate attention to duty; allegations or rumors of an individual's involvement with usage; unexplained disappearance from station house of property from personal lockers, vouchered property, and office equipment; and observation of a department member's associates.

Procedures for Control

Closely supervise subordinates in the field to insure the proper handling of arrests and searches.

Establish strict procedures for searches and the recording of evidence. Immediate search in presence of station house supervisor and recording of evidence should be made. Supervisor should issue a receipt for evidence that the arresting officer can place in his memo book.

Hold frequent conferences with superior officers and community groups to obtain information related to suspected practices in narcotics enforcement.

Initiate frequent independent or parallel observations of narcotic locations and of suspected officers.

Frequently review individual records to determine suspicious trends in arrests, dispositions, and investigative results.

Train members in current departmental procedures and policies.

Hold periodic, unannounced locker inspections to discover the unlawful withholding of evidence or contraband.

Superior officer review all narcotic arrests, especially those that are dismissed in court.

The examples used above were from a draft of a manual developed by the New York City Police Department (McCormack and Ward, 1979:27). This does not mean that they cannot be used by smaller departments. They give an idea of what to look for and how to possibly control the incidence of these behaviors. Obviously, the larger the department and the community where the department is located will influence the opportunities for corruption and misconduct. However, each Internal Affairs unit should be able to develop such a working manual for its own agency.

Undermining Group Support

Every occupational group socializes new members into the group. These occupational groups can create informal rules concerning deviant (rule breaking) behavior. The social isolation of the American law enforcement community and their withdrawal into their own group for support-group solidarity creates a situation whereby the law enforcement officer becomes subject to intense peer group pressure. This peer group can supply the rationalizations for corrupt acts. Some of the more common rationalizations are: law enforcement is a low paying job; these are just fringe benefits or perks of the job; it is covered by insurance; these people like the police; they are respectable people; it is "clean money;" everybody does it; if you don't do it, nobody will trust you; he is a criminal and it is illegal money, etc. The end result can be that the new officer is provided with a list of "safe" or tolerated patterns of corruption and misconduct. Couple this with the acknowledged "Code of Silence" known to be common in American law enforcement agencies and problems can occur.

What we can have in a law enforcement agency is a situation whereby the deviant officer (engaging in corruption or misconduct) is encouraged by the protection of his peers and the group's deviant set of values that supports the "Code of Silence." The group can also isolate and ostracize those who do not support the deviant values. Fortunately, the same group which can support deviant values can be channeled to support nondeviant values.

High Recruitment Standards

The first step in creating a peer group that would support nondeviant values is to ensure that all officers selected meet high recruitment standards, especially for honesty and integrity. Those departments that do not select suitable applicants soon pay the price. There have been at least two recent examples of agencies being forced to relax standards and the price they paid for this action (Dellatre, 1995).

In 1980, Miami, Florida, under pressure to recruit minority candidates, adopted a policy that 200 new police officers be hired immediately. Eighty percent of these new recruits were to come from the minority community. Little if any background checks were conducted on these new applicants. In addition, these new recruits were badly trained and negligently supervised. The background checks that were done and their police academy instructors' reports revealed that many were unsuited for police work. The end result was that by 1988, a third were fired and twelve members of the group, known as the "River Cops," were convicted of crimes ranging from drug trafficking to murder. Many had joined the police department in order to engage in drug trafficking.

This same scenario was repeated in Washington, D.C. some ten years later. Congress threatened to withhold $430 million unless 1,800 new police officers were hired. The Metropolitan Police Department hired 1,471 new officers in 1989 and 1990. In order to accomplish this, the department suspended the normal procedures for applications and lowered the passing grade on the entrance exam to 50 percent. Background investigations were conducted over the phone and FBI criminal records checks were ignored. Dellatre (1995) reports that some of the applicants were incarcerated at the time and they received their parole denial letters at the same time that they received notices that they were admitted to the police academy.

By 1994, one hundred of the officers in the newly hired group had been arrested for crimes, including drug trafficking, rape, and murder. Approximately 100 of these new officers are included in the 185 Metro officers who cannot be used as credible trial witnesses because of their bad records.

Other departments have undergone massive hiring programs, including the New York City Police Department which hired 11,000 new officers in the past three years. Dellatre fears that they will undergo the same experience as Miami and Washington, D.C.

Realistic Training Programs

Young officers must be aware of what they will or may face in the field. Corruption and misconduct must be candidly discussed. The **Law Enforcement Code of Ethics** must be an integral part of this training. However, it must be recognized that peer group socialization is an *ongoing* process. The path to corruption is often a gradual process. Therefore, undermining group support cannot be limited to "rookies." There must be a continuous in-service training program dealing with both the issues of corruption and misconduct and the **Code.**

Effective Leadership

The leaders must provide a role model for the entire department. A number of corrupt police departments have been reformed by able and honest administrators who have set the tone for the police peer group. The administrator who fails to acknowledge that corruption does or may exist in the agency, resists agency self-examination, and is reluctant to change conditions which encourage corruption is creating agency conditions conducive to corruption.

Increasing the Risk

If the peer group can be enlisted in the control of corruption, this will increase the risk for the "deviant" officer. If the officer contemplating an act of corruption or misconduct understands that he or she will not receive support or tolerance from his/her peers, this is often enough to deter the act. This is a positive approach. Unfortunately, some negative actions must be taken even when the peer group supports nondeviant values.

Internal Policing

Obviously, not every agency is large enough to have a separate unit for internal affairs. However, someone must be responsible for internal policing in every police department regardless of size. The internal policing policy must be based on two concepts. The first is that all complaints against officers, especially those involving serious misconduct or corruption, should be handled and investigated with the same tenacity and techniques as would be used against any suspected violator. The agency does not want to be criticized as having one set of rules for officers accused of misconduct and crimes and another when "citizens" are involved. The second basic concept is that the investigation should not stop even if the officer resigns. The matter must be resolved. The officer who chooses to resign may be guilty of a crime and may need prosecution. This will also prevent the practice common in some states whereby officers who resign under investigation are hired by other agencies.

Proactive or Reactive Internal Policing

A decision must be made whether or not the agency is to pursue a proactive or reactive policy of corruption control or even a combination of both approaches. Reactive control is confined to the investigation of complaints from citizens, victims, officers, other outside sources, etc. Obviously, complaints would also be investigated in a proactive approach. However, in a proactive approach the internal policing unit would seek out corrupt officers and check on corruption-producing conditions.

There are disadvantages to both approaches. In a strictly reactive policy, the actual likelihood of risk of discovery is very low. The police bureaucracy often presents a significant obstacle for anyone wishing to register a complaint on an officer. A strictly reactive policy usually leads to the conclusion that any corrupt officers identified are "rotten apples."

There are also several disadvantages to a proactive policy. For one, the "headhunters" charged with investigating fellow officers may one day be their partners or superiors. Several agencies in an attempt to deal with this make a tour in Internal Affairs mandatory for all midlevel managers. This may be a good solution because officers assigned to investigating other officers for long periods of time sometimes cease to be fair and objective investigators. Others have dealt with this problem by making it a mandatory assignment for promotion from sergeant to lieutenant.

Another disadvantage of the proactive approach is that it does not take long to create a sense of paranoia in the agency. Police organizations, because of the myriad number of rules and regulations, are often punishment-oriented bureaucracies. If a very active proactive Internal Affairs unit is added to this punishment-oriented atmosphere, paranoia runs rampant. Most of the studies on police stress have found that the majority of the police stress comes from the agency. It may be just as bad on the individual officer to work in a corrupt organization as to work in an organization whose goal is to be 100 percent corruption and misconduct free and works hard at accomplishing that goal, primarily through proactive Internal Affairs. Nevertheless, unless an outside agency is used to investigate corruption and misconduct, the agency must use some proactive strategies to increase the risk of corruption.

Proactive Strategies

Early Warning System. The IACP, in a 1989 publication produced for the Department of Justice, *Building Integrity and Reducing Drug Corruption in Police Departments,* suggested an Early Warning System to identify potential problem officers, integrity breakdowns, and management weaknesses. They recommend that data be gathered in at least four categories: officer complaints, assignment, shift or tour, and report types. Although complaints on officers will be collected, the system is not unduly focused on the individual officer because it examines the assignment and shift for a possible explanation of the complaint. For example, some assignments, irregardless of the officer, may receive certain types of complaints. Officers working vice may receive numerous entrapment complaints as well as officers working drug units may receive an inordinate number of excessive force complaints. That certainly does not mean that if the same officers working these assignments keep receiving complaints that there is not a problem.

The Early Warning System would routinely gather data from the following reports: (1) any discharge of a firearm, whether accidental or duty-related; (2) excessive use of force reports; (3) any motor vehicle damage; (4) any loss of equipment; (5) injured on duty reports; (6) use of sick leave in excess of five days, or a regular pattern of using one or two sick leave days over long periods; and (7) all complaints, including supervisory reprimands and other disciplinary actions. I would also add all reports on resisting arrests and assaulting an officer. These are very good reports to identify "violent men" or officers needing additional training.

The authors were quick to point out that any of the seven reports by themselves do not imply corruption or misconduct, but they could point out a trend or indication of a problem. For example, extended sick leaves and injuries are not incidents of misconduct, but they may point out an officer in need of medical, psychological, or social intervention.

Undercover Police Officers. Officers known for their "honesty" or rookie officers can be recruited to act as the "eyes and ears" of the internal policing unit. Obviously, when this practice becomes known, it is going to raise the paranoia level of the organization. I would suggest that it only be used in those departments with a history of corruption and an entrenched "Code of Silence."

Solicitation of Anonymous Complaints From Officers. Anonymous complaints from citizens or officers can be very useful in a proactive strategy against corruption and misconduct. However, they should be treated with objectivity and fairness to the officer identified in the complaint. They are not to be assumed to be true. Nevertheless, anonymous complaints from officers provide a vehicle whereby an officer can identify a deviant coworker without suffering any ill effects from the peer group.

Corruption Patrols. A substantial part of the proactive Internal Affairs unit should be spent in patrolling and monitoring possible corruption locations. Known "shot" houses, gambling locations, areas where prostitution are known to occur, bars, and the other potential indicators of a problem identified earlier must be monitored.

Interviews of Arrestees and Individuals Who Work in Corruption Assignments. The Internal Affairs unit should conduct random interview with arrestees and individuals who work in corruption high assignments such as vice and narcotics.

"Turn Arounds." A tactic that is usually abhorrent to most police officers is the use of "turn arounds." That is, granting immunity to corrupt officers for testimony against other officers or using them as undercover agents. The department using "turn arounds" can expect damaging publicity as soon as their use is made public. This tactic should only be used as a last ditch effort against entrenched corruption where the "Code Of Silence" is pronounced. However, "turn arounds" and undercover officers can greatly reduce the incidence of corruption if judiciously used.

Integrity Tests. Another tactic that brings on adverse publicity from both within and without the police organization is the use of integrity tests. This means creating artificial situations to give police officers the opportunity to commit crimes. Obviously, this tactic should also be used judiciously and sparingly.

Examples of integrity tests that have been used are:

1. Students or officers posing as drunks to see if money could be stolen by police officers or jail officials.

2. Wallets containing money or other valuables turned over to officers for safekeeping and return to owners.
3. Planting money or other valuables in illegally parked or abandoned vehicles.
4. Routing packages of supposed narcotics to officers who were led to believe the narcotics are real.
5. Sting Operations—Setting up businesses as fronts; pornographic shops, illegal gambling and drinking establishments, legal establishments operating illegally, to see if police officers will accept payoffs.

Chapter 10

SUMMARY

We began this book with the presentation of four questions: (1) Is law enforcement a profession? (2) Can law enforcement officers be professional? (3) What forms of behavior are the major law enforcement ethical violations? (4) Can these ethical violations be controlled? I do not believe that law enforcement is a profession as of yet. However, I believe that law enforcement officers can be professional in their behavior. I believe that this is a more realistic and achievable goal. They can be professional if their behavior conforms to a Code of Ethics. We then examined the current **Law Enforcement Code of Ethics** to see if it could be used as a model for professional behavior. The answer was yes it could be such a model.

We then examined the forms and patterns of ethical violation which could occur in a law enforcement agency. The forms and patterns of unethical behavior could occur in a police agency. Hopefully, all of them would not occur in any one police agency; but, unfortunately that has happened on occasion. We then examined what the author believes is the only way to control corruption and misconduct. It will take a three-pronged approach directed at (1) Decreasing the opportunity, (2) Undermining peer group support for these forms and patterns of unethical behavior, and (3) Increasing the risk of engaging in these activities.

Assuring police ethical behavior will not be an easy task, but the task is worth the effort. The author believes that the current ethical crisis in law enforcement must be resolved and we must begin the task. I hope that this small text will be helpful in this endeavor. Law enforcement officers and executives should also remember the following points as they strive to eradicate unethical behavior.

POLICE CORRUPTION EXISTS ONLY WHERE IT IS TOLERATED BY THE POLICE OFFICERS THEMSELVES. ONLY THE POLICE PEER GROUP CAN PERMIT UNETHICAL BEHAVIOR AND ONLY THE POLICE PEER GROUP CAN ELIMINATE IT.

EVERY LAW ENFORCEMENT OFFICER MUST RECOGNIZE THE HAZARDS OF CORRUPTION AND BE PREPARED TO FACE IT.

EACH LAW ENFORCEMENT OFFICER HAS THE INDIVIDUAL RESPONSIBILITY FOR MAINTAINING THE INTEGRITY OF HIS/HER AGENCY.

A LAW ENFORCEMENT OFFICER SHOULD AVOID ALL UNETHICAL ACTS BECAUSE THEY ARE WRONG, NOT BECAUSE OF ANY FEAR OF DEPARTMENTAL ACTION OR CRIMINAL PROSECUTION.

REFERENCES

Barker, Thomas (1986). "White Knights, Grass Eaters, and Rogues," presented at the *American Society of Criminology Annual Meeting*, Atlanta, GA.

Barker, Thomas, Hunter, R.D., and Rush, J.P. (1994). *Police Systems and Practices: an Introduction.* Englewood Cliffs, NJ: Prentice-Hall.

Barker, Thomas and Julian Roebuck (1973). *An Empirical Typology of Police Corruption: A Study in Organizational Deviance.* Springfield, IL: Charles C Thomas.

Carter, David L. and D.K. Dearth (1984). "An Assessment of the Mission," Texas Police Department. Unpublished Consultant's Report.

Carter, David L. and D.W. Stephens (1991). "An Overview of Issues Concerning Police Officer Drug Use," in Thomas Barker and David Carter, Eds. *Police Deviance*, 2nd ed. Cincinnati, OH: Anderson Press.

Commonwealth v. Lewin. 542 N.E. 2nd 275 Mass, 1989.

Delattre, Edwin J. "What is this noble (and elusive) concept we call integrity?" *Law Enforcement News*, July 20, 1995.

Hoy, V.L. (1982). "Research and Planning," in B. Garmire ed., *Local Government Public Management*, 2nd ed. Washington, DC: International City Management Association.

International Association of Chiefs of Police (1981). *Police Ethics*, Training Key 295. Gaithersberg, MD: IACP.

Kania, Richard E. (1988), "Should We Tell Police to say 'Yes' to Gratuities?" *Criminal Justice Ethics* (Summer/Fall). pp. 37-49.

Klockers, C.B. (1980). "The Dirty Harry Problem," *The Annals*, 452 (November): 34-47.

Knapp Commission (1973). *The Knapp Commission Report on Police Corruption.* New York: George Braziller.

Law Enforcement News (May 31, 1995). New York: John Jay College of Criminal Justice.

Marx, Gary T. (1985). "Who Really Gets Stung? Some Issues Raised by the New Police Undercover Work," in F.A. Elliston and Michael Feldberg, Eds., *Moral Issues in Police Work.* Totowa, NJ: Rowan and Allenheld.

McAlary, M. (1987). *Buddy Boys: When Good Cops Turn Bad.* New York: G.P. Putnam's Sons.

National Advisory Commission on Criminal Justice Standards and Goals (1973). *Police.* Washington, DC: GPO.

Ostrom, Elinor, Roger Parks and Gordon Whitaker (1978). *Patterns of Metropolitan Policing.* Cambridge, MA: Ballinger.

Pistone, J.D. (1987). *Donnie Brasco: My Undercover Life in the Mafia.* New York: Nail Books.
Sapp, Allen D. (1991). "Sexual Misconduct by Police Officers," in Tom Barker and David Carter Eds., *Police Deviance,* 2nd ed., Cincinnati, OH: Anderson Publishing Co.
Sherman, L. (1978). *Scandal and Reform: Controlling Police Corruption.* Berkeley, CA: University of California Press.
Skolnick, Jerome (1982). "Deception by Police," *Criminal Justice Ethics,* 1(2), (Summer/Fall): 40–50.
Stitt, B.G. and G.G. James (1985). "Entrapment an Ethical Analysis," in Elliston, F.A. and M. Feldberg (eds.). *Moral Issues in Police Work.* Totowa, NJ: Rowan and Allanheld.
U.S. Department of Justice (1978). *Prevention, Detection, and Correction of Corruption in Local Government.* Washington, DC: Department of Justice.
Ward, Richard and McCormack, Robert (1979). *An Anti-Corruption Manual for Administrators in Law Enforcement.* New York: John Jay Press.
Walker, Samuel (1983). *The Police in America: An Introduction.* New York: McGraw-Hill.
Witham, Donald C. (1985). *The American Law Enforcement Chief Executive: A Management Profile.* Washington, DC: Police Executive Research Forum.

INDEX

A

Avenging angel syndrome, definition, 19

B

Barker, Thomas, 11, 25, 41, 49, 79, 80
Bars, control police corruption and misconduct, 60–62
Bottle clubs, control police corruption and misconduct, 60–62

C

Cabarets, control police corruption and misconduct, 60–62
Canons of police ethics, 28
    free meals, 28–29
    gifts and favors, 28
Carter, David L., 48, 49, 79, 80
Carter, Jimmy, 16
Chimel v. California, 12
Code of Ethics (*see also* Law enforcement Code of Ethics)
    definition, 5
    need of for law enforcement, 5
    procedures, example, 57
    promotion ethical behavior by, 5–6
    purpose of, 5
Confidentiality, by law enforcement officers, 17
Construction sites, control police corruption and misconduct, 62–63
Contempt of cop citation, definition, 19
Corrupt practices, 37–42
    as systematic, 40
    corrupt groups, 40
        typical patterns of corruption practiced by, 40
    corrupt officers as "rotten apples," 37–40
    corrupt police departments, 40–41
        categories officers existing in, 41–42
    findings of Knapp Commission, 39
    police work as morally dangerous, 37–38
    rotten apple officers (*see* Rotten apple officers)
    "scores" as one time events, 37
    types of, 37–38
    use judgment when to write citations, 38–39
Corruption and misconduct control, 55–76
    at bars, grills, cabarets, and bottle clubs, 60–62
    at construction sites, 62–63
    at hotels and restaurants, 63
    considerations in eradicating unethical behavior, 77–78
    corruption hazards and indicators, 60
    decreasing the opportunity, 55–70
        educating the public, 59
        increased supervision, 60
        policy development, 55–70
        procedures, 57–59
        stance of administrator, 55
        sustained action and monitoring hazards, 60–70
    efforts toward, 55, 77
    for gambling, 68
    for narcotics, 68–70
    for parking lots, 64
    for prostitution, 67
    for repair shops, garages, trucking companies, 64–65
    for traffic violations, 66
    for tow trucks, 66–67
    gypsy or unlicensed cabs, 65–66
    increasing the risk, 72–76

Corruption and misconduct control (*Continued*)
    internal policing, 72–73
    proactive or reactive internal policing, 73
  policy development notes
    difference policy and procedures, 57
    examples, 56–57, 58–59
  proactive corruption control, 73–74, 74–76
    corruption patrols, 75
    early warning system, 74
    integrity tests, 75–76
    interviews of arrestees, 75
    solicitation anonymous complaints from officers, 75
    strategies, 74
    "turn arounds," 75
    undercover police officers, 74–75
  reactive corruption control, 73–74
  rules and regulations defined, 58–59
Corruption hazards, indicators, and monitoring, 60–70
  of bars, grills, cabarets, and bottle clubs, 60–62
  of construction sites, 62–63
  of gambling, 68
  of gypsy or unlicensed cabs, 65–66
  of hotels and restaurants, 63–64
  of narcotics, 68–70
  of parking lots, 64
  of prostitution, 67
  of repair shops, garages, trucking companies, 64–65
  of tow trucks, 66–67
  of traffic violations, 66
Corruption of authority, 26–30
  canons of police ethics, 27
  free and discounted meals, 28–29
  free cups of coffee debate, 26–27
    opinions of, 27, 28
  free perks of the job, 28–30
    rationalizations of, 29–30
    revenge on businesses refusing, 29
  gifts and favors, 28
  table, 38
  types of, 26
Corruption policy example
  policy developed, 56
  purpose, 56
Criminal investigation, definition, 10

Criminal justice system
  purposes of, 11
  role law enforcement officers, 11–12

D

Danza, Tony, 16
Dearth, D.K., 79
Delattre, Edwin J., 79
Direct criminal activities, 35–36
  other crimes, 35–36
  related to drugs, 35–36
  table, 38
  types of, 35
Direct police services, definition, 9, 10
Dirty Harry, 12–13
Drinking on duty, 48
Drug use by law enforcement officers
  as recreational activity, 48
  increase in, 48
Drug-testing methodology, procedures, 58

E

Elliston, F.A., 79, 80
Entrapment, 50–51
  definition, 50
  objective test of, 50
  subjective test of, 50
Escobedo, 12
Ethical behavior law enforcement
  standards of, v
    model of, v
Ethical problems
  during Simpson trial, 5–6
  existence of a crisis, v
  questions critical to, v, 3
Extraordinary powers of arrest, definition, 9–10

F

Feldberg, Michael, 79, 80
Fixes, 34–35
  behavior patterns included, 34–35
  methods used, 35
  table, 38
Fragmented law enforcement, 11
Furhman, Mark, 5–6, 54

G

Garages, corruption and misconduct control, 64–65
Garmire, B., 79
Gratuities acceptance
 attitude public toward, 21
 the Code and, 20–21
Grills, corruption and misconduct control, 60
Gypsy cabs, control police corruption and misconduct, 65–66

H

Hester v. U.S., 12
Hotels, control police corruption and misconduct, 65–66
Hoy, V.L., 79
Hunter, R.D., 11, 79

I

Internal payoffs
 table, 38
 types of, 36
International Association of Chiefs of Police, 3
 characteristics law enforcement as profession, 3
 pros and cons of, 3–4

J

James, G.G., 50, 80

K

Kania, Richard E., 30, 79
Kickbacks
 definition, 30–31
 types of, 31
King, Rodney, 6, 43, 45
Klockers, C.B., 49, 79

L

Law enforcement
 as a profession, 3–5
  IACP statements regarding, 3
 code of ethical behavior, 5 (*see also* Code of Ethics)
 dominate features of, 11
 establishment of London Metropolitan Police, 4
 growth as an occupation, 4
 misconduct by, 5–6, 6–7
 objective of, 12
 professional (*see* Professional law enforcement)
 protection individual freedoms, 12–13
 question officers as professionals, 5–7
 respect for Constitution and Bill of Rights, 12–13
 standards for admission, 4
 training of, 5
Law Enforcement Code of Ethics (*see also* Code of Ethics)
 as integral part training programs, 72
 copy of, 8
 paragraph four, 23–24
  personal commitment of law enforcement officer, 24
  trust in law enforcement badge, 23–24
 paragraph one, 8, 9–13
  key concepts of, 10
  powers of officer, 9–10
  those subject to, 9–10
 paragraph three, 19–21
 paragraph two, 15–17
  copy of, 8, 15
  references to private life, 15
 use as model for professional behavior, 77
Law enforcement ethical violations, 25–36
 corrupt practices, 37–42 (*see also* Corrupt practices)
 police corruption, 25 (*see also* Police corruption)
 police misconduct, 43–54 (*see also* Police misconduct)
Law enforcement officer
 as a public official, 9–10, 10–22
 as example of master status, 15–16
 attributes of, 16–17
 avenging angel syndrome, 19
 control of personal feelings, 19
 definition, 9
 ethical violations by (*see* Police corruption)
 keeping information private, 17

Law enforcement officer (*Continued*)
  personal commitment to code of ethics, 24
  rights of as protectors, 12
    misuse of, 12
  role in criminal justice system, 11–12
  selective enforcement of traffic laws, 20
  services performed, 10
  the Code and acceptance of gratuities, 20–21
  trust of society in, 23–24
  types in corrupt police organizations
    example, 42
    grass eaters, 42
    meat eaters, 42
    rogues, 42
    straight shooters, 41
    White Knights, 41, 42
  use of discretion, 19–20
    in issuing citations, 20
Law enforcement support group, 7
  effective leadership, 72
  high recruitment standards, 71–72
    scenarios in past, 71–72
  realistic training programs, 72
  undermining group support, 70–72
    Code of Silence by, 70–71
    creation informal rules for deviant behavior by, 70
    peer group pressure by, 70
    rationalizations for corrupt acts, 70
Limited authority, 11
Local control, definition, 11
London Metropolitan Police, establishment of, 4

M

Mapp, 12
Marx, Gary T., 49, 50, 79
McAlary, M., 32, 79
McCormack, Robert, 80
Miranda, 12
Misconduct policy example
  policy developed, 56–57
  purpose of, 56

N

Narcotics, control police corruption and misbehavior, 68–70
Narcotics and/or drug enforcement
  corruption, example, 58
  misconduct, example, 59
National Advisory Commission on Criminal Justice Standards and Goals, 12

O

Opportunistic thefts
  definition, 31
  description, 31–32
  table, 38
Ostrom, Elinor, 79

P

Parking lots, control police corruption and misbehavior, 64
Parks, Roger, 79
Patrol, definition, 10
Pistone, Joseph D., 49, 80
Police (*see* Law enforcement)
Police behavior, realistic expectations of, 59
Police brutality
  definition, 43, 44
  examination officer using, 44
  reasons for, 44
  Rodney King incident, 43
  situations using force, 43–45
    punishment of certain groups and individuals, 44–45
    resistance of arrest and runaways, 45
    result of fear, 44
    to effect or complete arrest, 43
    verbal abuse and provocation provoking, 44
Police corruption
  definition, 25, 26
  gifts and favors article, 29
  material reward or gain from, 25
  patterns of, 26–36
    corruption of authority, 26–30
    direct criminal activities, 35–36
    fixes, 34
    internal payoffs, 36
    kickbacks, 30–31
    opportunistic thefts, 31
    protection of illegal activities, 33–35
    shakedowns, 32–33
    table of, 38

Police corruption (*Continued*)
    solicitation "police discount," 25
    types of, 25
Police lies and deceptions, 49–54
    accepted lies, 49–52
        criteria for, 52
        for undercover operations, 49–51
        problems associated with, 49–50
        purposes of, 49
        to the media or public, 51–52
        whoops raids, 51
    deviant lying, 53–54
        in support of illegitimate goals, 54
        in support of perceived legitimate goals, 53
        testifying, 53–54
    tolerated lying, 52–53
Police misconduct, 43–54
    drinking on duty, 48
    drug use, 48
    police brutality, 43–45 (*see also* Police brutality)
    police lies and deception, 49–54 (*see also* Police lies)
    sex on duty, 45–47 (*see also* Sex on duty)
    sleeping on duty, 47
Policy
    attitude formation of, 55–56
    corruption of, example, 56
    difference from procedures, 57
    misconduct, example, 56–57
Procedures
    corruption, example, 57
        Code of Ethics, 57
        Rules of Conduct, 57
    definition, 57
    difference from policy, 57
    misconduct, example, 58
Professional law enforcement
    characteristics of, 3
    disciplinary system, 4
    mechanisms to ensure conformance, 4
    minimum educational standard, 4
    question of, 3–5, 77
    summary, 77–78
    term professional as behavior, 5
Prostitution, control police corruption and misbehavior, 67
Protection of illegal activities, 33–34
    definition, 34
    source of protection money or goods, 34
    table, 38
    victimless crimes included, 34
Public official, definition, 9

R

Repair shops, control police corruption and misbehavior, 64–65
Restaurants, control police corruption and misbehavior, 63–64
Roebuck, Julian, 25, 79
Rotten apple officers, 37–40
Ruby Ridge fiasco, 6
Rules and regulations, uses of terms, 58–59
Rush, J.P., 11, 79

S

Sapp, Allen, 45, 79
Schmerber, 12
Sex on duty, 45–47
    categories behaviors, 45–47
        citizen-initiated sexual contacts, 46–47
        contacts with crime victims, 46
        contacts with juvenile offenders, 46
        contacts with offenders, 46
        nonsexual contact, 45–46
        sexual shakedowns, 46
        voyeuristic contact, 46
Shakedowns, 32–33
    costs of DUI shakedown, 33
    definition, 32
    taking bribes, 32
    table, 38
Sherman, L., 40, 80
Skolnick, Jerome, 50, 80
Sleeping on duty, 47
Stephens, D.W., 48, 79
Stewart, Potter, 43
Stitt, B.G., 50, 80

T

Terry v. Ohio, 12
Testifying
    definition, 53
    first appearance of, 53–54

Tow trucks, control police corruption and misbehavior, 66–67
Traffic control, definition, 10
Traffic violations, control police corruption and misbehavior, 66
Trucking companies, control police corruption and misbehavior, 64–65

U

Unlicensed cabs, control police corruption and misbehavior, 65–66
U.S. v. Leon, 12

W

Waco incident, 6
Walker, Samuel, 11, 80
Wallace, William, 9
Ward, Richard, 80
Whitaker, Gordon, 79
Whitman, Charles, 15
Witham, Donald C., 4, 80

Charles C Thomas
PUBLISHER • LTD.

Leader In Criminal Justice and Law Enforcement Publications

▶ denotes new publication

▶ Violanti, John M. & Douglas Paton—**POLICE TRAUMA:** Psychological Aftermath of Civilian Combat. '99, 276 pp. (7 x 10), 16 il., 14 tables.

▶ Nelson, Kurt R.—**POLICING MASS TRANSIT:** A Comprehensive Approach to Designing a Safe, Secure, and Desirable Transit Policing and Management System. '99, 224 pp. (7 x 10), 14 il.. $46.95, cloth, $33.95, paper.

▶ Kushner, Harvey W.—**TERRORISM IN AMERICA:** A Structured Approach to Understanding the Terrorist Threat. '98, 232 pp. (7 x 10), $49.95, cloth, $35.95, paper.

▶ Mendell, Ronald L.—**INVESTIGATING COMPUTER CRIME:** A Primer for Security Managers. '98, 198 pp. (7 x 10), 5 il., 7 tables, $44.95, cloth, $30.95, paper.

Lester, David—**THE DEATH PENALTY:** Issues and Answers. (2nd Ed) '98, 174 pp. (7 x 10), 11 tables, $41.95, cloth, $27.95, paper.

Scott, Edward M.—**WITHIN THE HEARTS AND MINDS OF PRISONERS:** An In-Depth View of Prisoners in Therapy. '98, 190 pp. (7 x 10), 7 il. $42.95, cloth, $29.95, paper.

Chapman, Samuel G.—**MURDERED ON DUTY:** The Killing of Police Officers in America. (2nd Ed.) '98, 218 pp. (7 x 10), 3 il., 22 tables, $47.95, cloth, $32.95, paper.

Carter, Gordon R. & Stephen M. Boyle—**All You Need to Know About DNA, GENES AND GENETIC ENGINEERING:** A Concise, Comprehensive Outline. '98, 146 pp. (7 x 10), 23 il., 2 tables, $22.95, (paper).

Palermo, George B. & Edward M. Scott—**THE PARANOID:** In and Out of Prison. '97, 208 pp. (7 x 10), $49.95, cloth, $37.95, paper.

Roberts, Albert R.—**SOCIAL WORK IN JUVENILE AND CRIMINAL JUSTICE SETTINGS.** (2nd Ed.) 97, 474 pp. (7 x 10), 1 il., 16 tables, $87.95, cloth, $69.95, paper.

Covey, Herbert C., Scott Menard & Robert J. Franzese—**JUVENILE GANGS. (2nd Ed.)** '97, 374 pp. (7 x 10), 7 il., 1 table, $69.95, cloth, $49.95, paper.

Hibbard, Whitney S. & Raymond W. Worring—**FORENSIC HYPNOSIS:** The Practical Application of Hypnosis in Criminal Investigations. (Rev. 1st Ed.) '96, 390 pp. (7 x 10), 15 il., 3 tables, $60.95, cloth, $39.95, paper.

Macdonald, John M.—**RAPE: CONTROVERSIAL ISSUES**—Criminal Profiles, Date Rape, False Reports and False Memories. '95, 218 pp. (7 x 10), $59.95, cloth, $41.95, paper.

Collins, John J.—**THE CULT EXPERIENCE:** An Overview of Cults, Their Traditions and Why People Join Them. '91, 142 pp. (7 x 10), $36.95, cloth, $24.95, paper.

▶ Ellis, John W.—**POLICE ANALYSIS AND PLANNING FOR VEHICULAR BOMBINGS:** Prevention, Defense and Response. '99, 318 pp. (7 x 10), 63 il., 4 tables.

▶ Moriarty, Laura J. & David L. Carter—**CRIMINAL JUSTICE TECHNOLOGY IN THE 21st CENTURY.** '98, 300 pp. (7 x 10), 1 il., 32 tables, $59.95, cloth, $46.95, paper.

▶ Drielak, Steven C.—**ENVIRONMENTAL CRIME:** Evidence Gathering and Investigative Techniques. '98, 248 pp. (7 x 10), 30 il., 2 tables, $51.95, cloth, $38.95, paper.

McKasson, Stephen C. & Carol A. Richards— **SPEAKING AS AN EXPERT:** A Guide for the Identification Sciences—From the Laboratory to the Courtroom. '98, 228 pp. (7 x 10), 26 il., $50.95, cloth, $37.95, paper.

Slovenko, Ralph—**PSYCHOTHERAPY AND CONFIDENTIALITY:** Testimonial Privileged Communication, Breach of Confidentiality, and Reporting Duties. '98, 660 pp. (6 3/4 x 9 3/4), 17 il., $79.95.

Barker, Tom—**EMERGENCY VEHICLE OPERATIONS:** Emergency Calls and Pursuit Driving. '98, 128 pp. (7 x 10), 4 tables, $35.95, cloth, $22.95, paper.

Garner, Gerald W.—**SURVIVING THE STREET:** Officer Safety and Survival Techniques. '98, 298 pp. (7 x 10), $49.95.

Palermo, George B. & Maxine Aldridge White— **LETTERS FROM PRISON: A Cry For Justice.** '98, 276 pp. (7 x 10), $55.95, cloth, $41.95, paper.

Schlesinger, Louis B. & Eugene Revitch—**SEXUAL DYNAMICS OF ANTI-SOCIAL BEHAVIOR. (2nd Ed.)** '97, 324 pp. (7 x 10), 4 il., 2 tables, $64.95, cloth, $49.95, paper.

Burpo, John, Ron DeLord & Michael Shannon —**POLICE ASSOCIATION POWER, POLITICS, AND CONFRONTATION:** A Guide for the Successful Police Labor Leader. '97, 350 pp. (7 x 10), $64.95, cloth, $49.95, paper.

Schlesinger, Louis B.—**EXPLORATIONS IN CRIMINAL PSYCHOPATHOLOGY:** Clinical Syndromes with Forensic Implications. '96, 366 pp. (7 x 10), 2 il., 10 tables, $77.95, cloth, $51.95, paper.

Barker, Tom—**POLICE ETHICS:** Crisis in Law Enforcement. '96, 94 pp. (7 x 10), 1 table, $36.95, cloth, $20.95, paper.

Chuda, Thomas J.—**A GUIDE FOR CRIMINAL JUSTICE TRAINING:** How to Make Training Easier for Security and Law Enforcement. '95, 156 pp. (7 x 10), 44 il., $40.95, cloth, $26.95, paper.

Germann, A. C., Frank D. Day & Robert R. J.Gallati—**INTRODUCTION TO LAW ENFORCEMENT AND CRIMINAL JUSTICE. (Rev. 31st Ptg.)** '88, 412 pp. (6 1/8 x 9 1/8), $31.95.

Books sent on approval • Shipping charges: $5.50 U.S. / $6.50 Canada • Prices subject to change without notice

Contact us to order books or a free catalog with over 800 titles
Call 1-800-258-8980 or 1-217-789-8980 or Fax 1-217-789-9130
2600 South First Street • Springfield • Illinois • 62704
Complete catalog available at www.ccthomas.com • books@ccthomas.com